PRAISE FOR AF

"I have read this *Artist of Love* cover to cover and I have to say, I've learned a great ...
It gave me so many deep insights into the feminine psyche. Whatever stage you are in
your relationships, I wish you an amazing journey into this beautiful, powerful book."

Richard Rudd
Author of *The Gene Keys: Embracing Your Higher Purpose*

"*Artist of Love* will unleash the sacred lover in you. It will challenge you, heal you,
and transport you into new dimensions of love and divinity. This book is a practi-
cal guide and melting pot of poetry—at the same time."

Chandresh Bhardwaj
Author of *Break the Norms: Questioning Everything You Think*
You Know About God and Truth, Life and Death, Love and Sex

"Madelyn Moon is a new leader in the world of romance and masculine/feminine
dynamics. She speaks with candor, humor, and wisdom to guide women back to
love. Starting with the foundation of self-love, Madelyn gives us the tools (both emotional and intellectual) to give and receive love without force or resistance. The lessons in this book are truly a gift."

James McCrae
Author of *Shit Your Ego Says: Strategies to Overthrow*
Your Ego and Become the Hero of Your Story

"This book quenches the thirst of a disembodied world by illuminating the energies of
feminine and masculine that abide in us all. Madelyn Moon offers insights for har-
monizing polarities while reclaiming the creative divinity that overflows every parti-
cle of reality and expresses itself at the heart of our relationships."

Mirabai Starr
Author of *Wild Mercy* and *Caravan of No Despair*

"Madelyn's weaving together of sacred theater, intimacy and polarity demonstrates
cutting edge methods for bringing our whole heart and revealing our true self in relationship. What an awesome approach to creativity as devotion. Every lover should
read this book."

Marya Stark
Award-winning vocalist, composer, producer,
performer, and multi-instrumentalist

"Madelyn Moon is a force. There aren't many people I meet that are truly the embodiment of the work they are doing in the world. Madelyn holds potent integrity & leads herself through the fire so she can do the same for others.

Her work around relational dynamics is powerful; it's fueled with love and delivered with grace. Curl up on the couch and devour this body of work, you will calibrate to a completely new place."

Samantha Skelly
Author of Hungry for Happiness: Stop Emotional
Eating and Start Loving Yourself

"There's no better teacher on the subject of bringing creative artistry into your romantic relationships than Maddy Moon. If you've laughed and learned from Maddy's impossibly witty and wise social videos, as we all have, then you'll love this deeper inquiry and instruction on how to bring the magic of creative artistry into your own relationships."

Dominick Quartuccio
Host of The Great Man Within Podcast

"Madelyn brings a wonderfully refreshing and creative approach to love and relationships. Her book is filled with poetic teachings and wisdom, relatable personal stories, and embodiment practices that encourage each of us to discover and share the unique archetypes within us."

Silvy Khoucasian
Relationship Coach + Teacher

"Madelyn Moon reveals a new perspective on love and loving. Love as expression, love as art, love as an offering to the divine. Being and becoming love. *Artist of Love* unlocks secrets to creating life-changing depth, closeness and connection in every relationship. Love that lights up the world."

Dawn Cartwright
Neo-Tantra Visionary

"Madelyn has created a magical dance of play, art, and insight with her words. Her readers will walk away with both inspiration and easily understood steps to immediately take her teachings from their heads deep into their bodies and hearts. Rarely in the same book do we get to read art and experience art, all while being taught how to make our own art — we do just that with *Artist of Love*."

Traver Boehm
Author of Man UNcivilized: The Guidebook for Men and
Women to Understand the Emerging Paradigm of Masculinity

ARTIST
L*of*VE

MADELYN MOON

ISBN: 979-8-9866165-1-3 (Paperback)
ISBN: 979-8-9866165-0-6 (eBook)

Edited by James Ranson
Cover design by Vanessa Mendozzi
Cover image by Violeta Meyners
Interior design by KUHN Design Group

maddymoon.com

To every teacher, mentor, guide, friend and beloved that has taken me deeper into the lessons that make life worth living.

CONTENTS

INTRODUCTION

INTRODUCTION

know something about you. Maybe it's a secret you've only shared with your best girlfriends. Maybe everyone you know knows it, too. Or maybe you've barely admitted it to yourself. Either way, I know it's your truth: *you want to be in love*. Madly, wildly, utterly in love.

Maybe you've found someone special, or perhaps you're entrenched in the wild west of singledom. Either way, there's something missing. That sparkly sensation you remember at the start of courtship, that enticing land of possibility, that fluttery feeling in the tummy when he looks at you in a certain way…where did it all go?

Somehow along the way, you have found yourself shapeshifting from *who you are in love* into *what is expected of you in love*. That wild, free-spirited woman you remember once being became a reserved, responsibility-burdened roommate. The larger-than-life seductress you used to be has gradually fallen to the wayside in pursuit of pleasing a partner over yourself.

Perhaps you're single but feeling like each heartbreak leaves you less and less hopeful. Too afraid to fall in love again, but too bored to stay single forever, you're stuck in the in-between land. You crave passion, romance, depth, and shimmering chemistry—but you can't seem to find it. You're even a little scared of finding it. What happens if it's taken away?

Relationship has been your deepest craving, and yet your biggest pain point. *Why hasn't love worked out for me like it has for so many others? Why do I keep matching with the same type of half-hearted man? Would I still be with my ex if I could have just become more of what he wanted? Does my husband really see me? Does he still love me the way he did when we met? Why don't I feel his adoration for me, and my devotion for him? Why don't I want to have sex with him like I used to? Am I not being responsible enough for my own pleasure?*

You've been looking for answers. You've been on a search to not only bring back the pulse of love, but to make love last longer. To find real commitment, integrity, and devotion.

Yet everywhere you search, you stumble upon reasons why you're not behaving in the way a woman should behave if she wants to be attractive to a man. Be softer, the books say. Be sweeter, the teachers say. Open your heart more, the embodiment troupes proclaim.

But I'm doing all of that! you retort.

Do it bigger, better, more! they say.

While there is certainly deep value in softness, sweetness and an open heart (you'll be learning a lot more about this throughout this book), the real key you're looking for—deep within—is not one that makes you believe you're to blame for not having romance. The real teaching is one that helps you realize you were never to blame—and you're not a project to fix. You are a woman to *liberate*.

The reason you haven't felt fulfilled in your relationships is because you've gotten a little lost in the game of love. You've been trying all the tricks of the trade to become more "womanly"—and they've led you to feeling like a failure of sorts. So…if that feeling resonates, I've got beautiful news for you. I understand you, and I know *exactly* where you're coming from.

You don't want to contort yourself into what the world says is the perfect women, the ideal wife, the glorified babe, or even the modern-day open-hearted goddess. You're tired of meeting the standards that men laid out for you ten thousand years ago. You want to make your *own* standards for love. You want to find blossoming, heartfelt love inside of your *freedom*—not outside of it.

The specific flavor of love you're desiring isn't found inside of a relationship at *first*—that comes with time. The first place that love can be found is within yourself—but more specifically, within your liberation. When you create, liberate, and express the vastness of who you are, you will fall madly, wildly, and utterly in love. With yourself, with life and with others. You've unlocked the dam on your truth, and what comes gushing out is rich with color. It's not always sweet, but that's part of the fun.

If you're hungry for a rich AF love life, it's important to know that the fantastical love you're looking for lies in *you bringing more of yourself to the table—not less*. You are the key to the expansive, sexy, polarized relationship you want. Your sensitivity, heart, quirkiness, dreams, ambitions, loudness, lostness, strength, weakness, fire, water, earth and air... it is all needed in your relationship.

Let's take a look at an alternative world, with a completely different way of existing as a woman.

A world where...

* The radiance of your heart shines like a million suns, magnetizing dream partners and friendships in every direction.

* You have a sexual fire that initiates deeper, darker, juicer, plumper love with a masculine soul-mate of your dreams.

* Every day you wake up and feel like a different woman, with exciting, fertile ambitions *and* the ability to take action on them.

* You effortlessly tap into your ever-flowing stream of creativity straight from the seat of your womb and the pulse of your heart.

* You say what you want, think what you think, do whatever you do and question *none* of it. You trust yourself without a shadow of a doubt.

* You are fully alive with emotions and passionately, easefully embody everything without attaching to anything. You experience true freedom in the skin you're in.

You might be reading that list and thinking, "Yes, that's great for other women, but that kind of life is just for them—the *chosen* ones."

Oh yes, the elusive chosen women.

The women who can wear a trash bag and look like supermodels. The women who leave toxic relationships easily because they can get a better match within days. The women who somehow look even more beautiful when they cry. The women who make millions of dollars because they manifest money through their orgasms. The women who have big loving families they can count on to support them when all else fails. The women who have white skin, straight teeth, skinny waists, and large social media followings. The women who have all the men's heads turning the moment they walk into any room.

You may think these women inherently have a secret sauce that is seemingly unavailable to you, but they don't. They might have privilege because of their skin, beauty or family of origin, yes—but freedom to exist as the woman you were born to be comes only from an invisible place, deep within the womb. It comes from the seat of your power.

The only true difference from the "chosen ones" and you, my lovely reader, is that the former has connected with *their* freedom of feminine expression.

They may have had the privilege of being raised in an environment that supported their freedom from birth, or maybe they also had to go through all of the steps to find their own expression under years of repression and toxic relating. Maybe it was given to them, or maybe they earned it — either way, they found it. And when you observe them, you *feel* it.

What you're feeling isn't beauty — it's radiance. And radiance is only ever something that's cultivated inside and pours outside, directly from the heart. You can quite literally see how much permission a woman gives herself to be in her fullest expression by experiencing how *open* she is. You feel magnetized to her, and you can feel how she's a magnet in general: for love, attention, desire and company. Not because she was born that way, but because she has taken back her power. She owns her own life, art and expression. She has sovereignty and nobody — *NOBODY I TELL YA!* — can take it away from her.

But you don't have to be "chosen" by some external part of life or society or the universe to be a woman like that. This is not about others choosing you. This is about *you* choosing you. You are the chosen one because *you are the one choosing*.

And the way that you choose isn't simply by thinking of a new choice. It's much more fun than that. The way that you physically, viscerally embody the act of choosing *you* is through becoming an artist with the pulsing, internal world of yours. Let your insides come outside in a language only you can speak. Be innovative with your hidden world. Bring your truth into your love life, your relationships and into romance herself. Become the energy you wish to experience.

Your romantic relationship hasn't been dull and struggling because it's not the right one — it's because *the full you is missing*. Your version of an out-of-the-box woman is literally what brings fresh, vibrant life into your sex life forever and ever. When you keep finding new ways to unleash more of your heart in any given moment, there is consistently more of yourself present in a relationship. When you make it your living, breathing job to bring different pieces of yourself back online, it's essentially like your partner gets to be with a different woman every single night—but it's always you.

The truth is, for as long as you hide all of your sparkly, erotic, brave, limelight mojo (especially in relationship to your lover), your partnership is going to feel drab.

While chemistry may have been easier at the beginning when everything was new and exciting, it's normal for it to start to fade when you merge your life together and start living in sync. This is, interestingly, when all your old behaviors of feeling "too much" may start to come back and you slowly find yourself shrinking smaller as the relationship becomes more of a long-term thing. This is a problem for many couples, which is why once they start getting to the *real* commitment and the *real* depth, they want to bounce out.

I've often heard my students say things like…

"If he was really the one, I would still want to pounce on him."

"If he was meant for me, we would still have chemistry and our sex life would still be as delicious as day one."

"He's no longer putting in any effort! I don't want to marry a lazy man!"

"I can't feel my own self nearly as much when I'm around him, so I should just be single."

But what if it wasn't all his fault?

What if this was totally, completely normal and simply required some artistry and skill-developing to resolve and reinvigorate?

And what if *you're* the powerful, erotic creatrix who can shift this dynamic by becoming a divine priestess of love?

If you want both a deep relationship and hot, hot sex, you're going to have to become to creatively embodied feminine being you were born to be. Not only for the relationship, but for the bright, etheric, all-encompassing, radiant woman you're destined to be. No more waiting—it's time to get to creating.

WHY TAKE A RISK IN LOVE?

A question that often comes up for any woman new to the idea of *being creative in love* is: why?

"Why go out of my way to *create* change in my partnership when my partner has no interest in doing the same for me?"

"Why change my ways now that I've created routine and stability with my partner? Won't it confuse him if I all of a sudden start acting in new ways?"

"What if I risk being violently shoved back into a box when he — or the world — feels threatened by my growth?"

"Why open my heart and risk being *exposed* or worse… *embarrassed?*"

Here are a few top reasons why the artistry of love is a two-birds-one-stone kind of situation, leading to a happier, healthier, more alive you as well as a deeper, richer, more joyful love life.

1. This is how you *heal* yourself.

You know how every time you feel jealousy, insecurity, anger, shame or guilt, you normally collapse? That is, you internalize your pain, make it mean that something is "wrong" with you, and fall into a pity party extravaganza? Yeah, that. With allowing your own expression to exist in artistic yet truthful ways, *that* can be a thing of the past.

The reason why most people internalize negative emotions is because they weren't taught how to channel their pain and turn it into something. Therefore, it simply sits inside of the body, growing bigger and uglier until it manifests as a big ol' resentful boulder in the heart.

When you learn how to demonstrate, manifest or channel your emotions, you finally—FINALLY—heal yourself in your emotional experience.

Instead of shaming or pushing down a completely valid emotion you're having, you bring it to the surface, honor it and even give it a voice. The experience of *creating* from a place you traditionally held shame around is one of the most magical self-help tools you will ever uncover.

And…it's the only way you can truly liberate yourself from that emotion. What you don't own, owns you.

This doesn't only go for negative emotions, but also positive ones! If you want to feel seen in your magnificence, eroticism, abundance and wealth—create from that place. Or, *manifest* what you desire from that place. Art is a wonderful way to support your visions, dreams and desires in coming true by creating as if it's already here.

2. This is how you go *deeper* in sex.

We all want more and better sex. But this usually doesn't just magically fall into your lap, especially if you've been with the same partner for a long period of time.

The thing that creates deeper, richer, more connected sex is actually two things: energy and depth.

There are thousands of different versions within you. Being creative in love means you're committed to exploring those parts of yourself through artistic expression. You're devoted to the part of you who is wolf just as much as you are devoted to the part of you who is lamb. You're devoted to your inner child as you are to your inner queen. Same for your sacred slut-ness and your divine mother-ness. You are all of it. And through ceremony, gifts, drama and dance, you can move between these archetypes, bringing more range of energy into your partnership.

There's nothing quite like playing on the full spectrum of the sexual realm. In my own partnerships, I've experienced the joys of being thrusted, spanked and tussled with like a ragdoll, and then tenderly worshiped with rose petals and oils like a goddess receiving her daily adorning. When I experience this variety from my partner, I fall even more madly in love.

And when he experiences my range from devoted wife to slutty high school cheerleader to angelic mother (even though I'm not a mother yet, this energy is accessible to all), he also falls even more madly in love with me.

When range is present in a relationship, you're able to play all over the spectrum with different parts of each other. The more parts available to meet, the more parts you get to love.

3. You'll *stop settling* for so-so relating.

Another reason why it's so crucial a woman learns how to *be* what she craves, is that many women are unconsciously starved for depth in their partners and will settle for anyone who offers even a morsel of it. Depth can look like financial security, stability, strength and other traditional male roles in a partnership. It's not wrong, at all, to want these things as a woman, but when you want them so badly, you'll stay in toxic, boring or unsatisfying relationships long past their due date just so that you have access to them (meanwhile your spirit is slowly, painfully dying).

To be clear, I'm not saying you need to leave your relationship if he's not taking you to the deepest depths and beyond. In fact, I'm encouraging the opposite—*demand* depth by *embodying* energy. *Take a stand* for the love you crave by *becoming* it.

If you've been clamping down on your desires, it's only natural your partner has no idea you want something different. On the other hand, if you've only been complaining, versus creating, that also makes it much less enticing for him to change. He's already let you down, so why change now?

This book will show you exactly how to bring the heat in a creative, inspiring way so you can truly see if your partnership can stand that test of time. If, after practice, they can't meet you where you want to go in your relationship, you'll be able to walk away knowing someone else can. You won't *need* them to supply you with merely a raindrop's worth of depth when you know you're deserving of an entire ocean.

4. This is how you *become* the woman who has it all.

You do not become the woman who has it all (including incredible sex, a dreamy relationship, a beautiful home, an abundant bank account and a sparkling, ever-evolving wardrobe) by simply "getting" it.

While it's a great theory to call in or manifest everything you want, it's not what will deeply, truly fulfill you as a woman.

(Trust me, I've had the dream home and life situation on paper, but was still left scratching my head due to feeling completely unmet and unexpressed as the woman I wanted to be.)

The kind of whole-bodied, knee-trembling, awe-inspiring life you're looking for comes through your individual creation of it... as well as your surrendering to it.

By *becoming* the very thing you want to have in your life, you end up healing your deepest wounds in love, which leaves you feeling whole, perfect and divinely feminine. Only from there can you begin to magnetize everyone who is truly able to meet you in that level of creative magnificence.

And you can't keep waiting for a magical, masculine man to show up and take you there. Because even if he did, something would still be missing. And not to mention, waiting for someone else to give you permission is just another patriarchal pattern that must be broken in order to have true sovereignty.

It's *you* that must venture into the great unknown. It's *you* who needs to become the thousands of women in the body of one. It's *you* who needs to create ceremony, express her fullest heart and make art.

The process of getting there is the reward—not just that final destination. Receiving these things are great—but the actual act of you embodying, creating and doing the thing is where the real transformation happens.

By becoming an artist of love, some of the constants you can expect to experience include:

* Waking up every morning to a closet full of colorful clothing and rich adornments for the many versions of yourself to choose from.

* Creating art (from videos to skits to dances to poetry) every single day to express the truth of your soul and blast that truth in the world for all to see.

* Deep, heart-opening sex where the bedroom is a literal temple and you feel divinely held in love.

* Easily attract the highest caliber of friendships and let those who are dragging you down or sucking your life force energy fall away (without guilting yourself).

* Knowing how to *instantly* spark sexual chemistry, hunger and attraction with romantic partners when your daily routine is getting too consistent or monotonous.

* Busting out of the box society has tried to cram you into and unveiling the wild, unabashed, eclectic YOU.

If you've been peeking over the fence at all these other women who seem to have a never-ending sparkle in their life, decide it's your turn to discover the depths within your own creative capabilities.

Are you ready to re-enliven your sex life? Breathe fresh life into dating experiences? Learn new ways to reveal to your partner the heartache of him picking up his phone more times than he looks at you? Surrender to the oceanic flow of love that has always been coursing through your veins?

Do you want to discover more of yourself, *truly*? To create from the very essence of your womb? To open your heart in a million and one ways? To be scared and do the thing anyways?

All of the things you currently feel hopeless about—your boring sex life, the gray blanket of "blah" over your heart, your inability to feel creative, your lack of skills when it comes to explaining your needs in relationship, the constant butting of heads with your beloved, the paralysis by analysis tumor growing in your psyche—will be dramatically, theatrically, and colorfully transmuted by becoming an artist of love.

Let's lift the dam that's currently blocking your watery flow of expression, and lead you into feeling a whole lot more like *you*.

ARTIST OF LOVE
READER'S MANUAL

This is a book about recreating yourself through the power of creativity, art and love. About giving a voice to *all* the pieces and parts of yourself—not just the ones that are considered socially acceptable.

Everything about you that's been offline gets to come back online. And it's going to feel really fucking good.

While this book is about liberating the many flavors of *woman* existing within you—this book is also about love and partnership (specifically, how love is a gateway *to* those many flavors). The conversation of relationships will be woven into the fabric of this entire book simply because your romantic life is a central gateway to deeper self-discovery, art and liberation.

Not only that, but every time you look at how you exist in a relationship, you're simultaneously getting a peek into how you are in all of life. Your relationships are reflections for everything—your self-worth, confidence, power, strength, creativity, reactivity, resilience, devotion, sexuality, bounteousness and more.

Love is your secret weapon as an artist because relationships will *always* give you opportunities to open, go deeper and remain devoted in love. They're a divine mirror to the artist in you, and the further you can go in intimacy, the further you can go in the world itself.

Do I need to be in a committed relationship to get the most out of this book?

No ma'am! If you happen to be single, this book will be a fantastic resource for you as you prepare yourself for the relationship of your dreams and become the woman you want to be for him.

Think of this as one of the ways you are preparing for his arrival into your life. This is you preparing your holy temple for all of the goodness to come; and by doing this work *now* you are manifesting a partner that can meet you here. The deeper you go into this work as a woman, the thicker the line you're drawing in the sand for anyone who is *not* able to have this kind of healthy, exquisite, artistic relationship.

Is this book just for heteronormative people?

The teachings you will discover in this book apply beautifully to all genders, orientations, identities and relationship pairings. Remember, this is a book about *dropping* the labels and boxes you have found yourself in, so I encourage you to respect and honor the identities you have bravely claimed while also knowing that—as an artist—you are limitless.

For continuity and clarity, I will be speaking directly to women, using she/her pronouns, and when I refer to her having a partner in a relationship, I will use he/him pronouns. Please substitute the pronouns that suit you and your partner, if you have one, best.

When I begin writing about feminine and masculine energies, please know that you have *both* of these—there would be no escaping it even if you tried. The gender you choose to go to bed with and the gender you identify with do not matter when it comes to whether or not you have feminine and masculine energies. You have both—always!

Do I need to be a creative person or artist to understand this book?

Everyone is an artist. Society has split people up into "right-brained" and "left-brained" people, but *everyone* has the ability to be creative and I encourage you, especially if you think you're not artistic, to recognize that you're made up of the same stuff as every other artist: blood, skin and bones.

Being an artist is about trust. Art is inherently risky because you're creating something out of nothing. If you're a left-brained person, you're most likely used to following a particular formula to achieve a desired result. Art isn't really like that.

Art requires you to step into the unknown and allow the journey itself to be the gift—not the outcome. If you can let yourself do a nice big trust fall with the universe, you're going to discover an entirely new, colorful, side of yourself. And with that, you'll inherently become better at taking risks in *all* avenues of life, but particularly your love life. The biggest creative risks are where the deepest rewards live.

What if I have trauma? Will this book be helpful for me?

This is a "yes and…" kind of answer. We all have trauma in some shape or form, but the severity and the amount of time that has passed will matter when it comes to how deep you will be able to go into the practices within this book.

This book is not a substitute for clinical and/or professional help. I advise you create a team of badass support for yourself so you can feel held as you move forward.

My own personal trauma has been tremendously supported and healed from discovering and becoming an artist of love, but this work can certainly be "too much too fast" if your nervous system isn't ready to have your heart exposed in the ways that will be shared in this book.

Everything throughout this book is written through the context that your nervous system is able to hold super, big expansive moments of creative leaps and bounds (in love and life) — and that you authentically enjoy the thrill of those moments. If you're not there *yet*, this might be an enjoyable read, but not something to jump head first into yet. I encourage you to trust your body's inherent wisdom and go slow if you don't think you're ready to reveal your inner artist's bleeding heart. *Everything happens in divine timing.*

Can men read this book?

Absolutely! Men are also artists of love.

That said, I will be writing directly to women throughout these pages, and the way a woman becomes an artist of love may be different from, let's say, a heteronormative male.

If you identify as a man, I recommend you read this book to understand and sympathize with the relational challenges most women must navigate to courageously liberate their truth, and to ponder how you can support the women in your life to become more expansive, creative and expressive in their endeavors.

And, you can most certainly, apply the practices and theories shared in this book to become your own artist of love.

PREPARING YOUR INSTRUMENT

Throughout this book you will be exploring many different tools, practices, exercises and modalities which may be new to you.

Just like many people use gemstones, tarot cards, pendulums or crystal balls as tools for understanding themselves and others more deeply, the most important instrument *you* have is your body.

Your body (including your voice, movements, and body *language*) creates the range of expression and depth of emotion your instrument is capable of. This is all you need in order to become an innovative, creative, heart-centered artist of love.

Actors spend much of their waking hours utilizing and training their bodies to become endless instruments, capable of feeling any emotion no matter how trivial or significant. They train their bodies to be open vessels, ready to be used for feeling the internal world of people whom they are not in real life. This requires emotional availability, imagination and courage. Actors who take their art seriously keep their body in a constant state of openness so that emotions can keep arising, teaching them more about how to embody characters and emote feelings. Every time they feel an emotion "in real life" they are able to translate it into their work. Therefore, the more available they are for life to penetrate them, the more skillful they are with their art.

Acting is one of my favorite tools for the artistry of love because it teaches you how to instantly move from "yourself" into a character, which essentially means, move from one emotion to another. Your emotional agility becomes *highly* trained, which is a skill every life artist should have. Your emotions as a woman will lead to your GREATEST art.

With all of this said, here are some things you can expect as we embark on this quest together:

Acting and Improvisation Exercises

By becoming an actor, you discover more of yourself. I will regularly invite you to do acting and improvisational techniques so that you can massage, fine-tune and open up your instrument. Think of these practices as *rehearsals* for the great drama of life. In order to know the how, when, what and why of the rest of the scene — you need to have it living in your body first! You need *practice*. Don't skip these.

Embodying Archetypes

Archetypes are characters or symbols that encompass and represent certain types of characters, experiences or identities that are familiar to the world. Throughout this book, you will learn about the four artist of love archetypes I have created, and how you can embody any of the four any time you please. You will learn skills for invoking each archetype so that you can bring them to your personal life, your relationship and your connection with the world itself.

Similarly to how becoming a *character* from a script can support you in discovering more of yourself, so do archetypes. By *fully* embodying the archetypes I will share with you, you can learn to amplify your natural gifts.

Dissecting Movie Scenes & Analyzing Characters

The best way to learn what it really looks like to become artistic with love, is to watch it happen. Since most of us aren't able to replay our fights to analyze later, we can learn through watching it happen in movies or shows.

I will use scenes and characters throughout this book to demonstrate how different people embody the artistry of love. Please do not worry about interrupting your reading experience to watch the scenes yourself; I will explain them, and any characters mentioned, in full detail so that you don't have to. (You are, of course, welcome to seek them out after you finish reading if you'd like to dive deeper!)

The important thing is to slow down around these parts of the book — they're very important. It's these very scenes I will write about that will teach you how to have deeper sex, artistry and love.

Learning Relationship Dynamics

There's a reason why the partner you feel the safest with also makes you feel the least safe. There's a reason why your sex was so hot and steamy when you first met but slowly, agonizingly faded the more familiar you became with each other. There's also a reason for why you simultaneously adore *and* feel maddened by your man's relationship with work and purpose.

You will be learning why you're no exception to these very common conundrums and mysterious paradoxes — and what to do about them to create steamier, sovereign, powerful attraction once again.

Feeling Weird

You're going to feel weird at times. You're going to make noises that aren't socially acceptable. You're going to overthink if you're doing something correctly. You're going to want to whisper instead of roar "just in case the neighbors hear you." You're going to feel uncomfortable, awkward and self-conscious.

Good. That's your wake-up call.

Your body was designed to do all of those things you may now consider weird: crawl, yell, sway, laugh, hiss, wail, growl and dance. Anytime you feel insecure about using your instrument in a different way, just remember, that insecurity belongs to *society* — not you. You are a wildly open goddess of creativity — and every time you do the thing that society tells you isn't proper, you're evolving as a woman. You're taking a stand for ancestors and future generations alike.

Shadow Exploration

Your shadow sides — meaning, the parts you've shut down because you've been told they're too bad, wrong, dark, inappropriate or damaging — are important here. They are welcome here.

I'm going to encourage you to look at some of your darker qualities, such as your jealousy, anger, insecurity, vengeance and/or deceitfulness. These parts of you are also messengers, and it's only when they're brought into the light that they can finally be free of the dark cloak of shame strangled around their neck and deliver to you the message that you need to receive.

At times, you may feel uncomfortable or challenged as you read this book. Pay specific attention to the moments that make your stomach turn, blood boil or knees shake. Behind every physical reaction is an emotional one. And wherever there is an emotional experience, there is big potential for creativity.

When you say "yes" to being an artist of love, you are saying yes to turning your pain into something personal as well as *purposeful*. Instead of letting resentment, longing, frustration or needs silently gnaw away at your heart, you commit to learning embodied ways of revealing your feelings as an offering — a gift.

Sometimes you'll make art to give to another. Sometimes you'll create art to reveal it to the world. And sometimes, your art may be something you need to just do — and it's in the *doing* of it that the healing is done.

When you merge creativity with emotion, all kinds of magic is possible.

To prepare for this journey, I invite you to put away other books so you can completely focus on the artistry of love. It can be challenging to devote your time and attention to learning only one thing in a world with millions of things to learn, but you'll be amazed by how much more you will receive from this book by going all in and reducing as many other distractions as possible.

Lastly, if you are in a relationship, it may be tempting from time to time to think that if you're going to do all of this work to become artistic, then your partner should too. That's a natural impulse, but not a helpful one. If you feel yourself start to direct your attention toward what your partner should or should not do, gently nudge yourself back into your own creative lane and remember that you're invoking your artistry as a woman for *you*. This is a part of your self-discovery, healing journey and you're becoming a better, deeper, wider, richer, more honest woman for it. This is how you claim you.

Don't wait. Let's dive in.

Part One

THE ARTISTRY
OF LOVE

THE ARTIST OF LOVE

An artist of love is she who is devoted to using her love life as a gateway to creativity, artistry and sacred expression. So being an artist of love means you're devoted to love above all. And I don't mean only love-and-light kind of love, but also the darker bits of life. Emotions like anger, jealousy, confusion, grief and rage are all also forms of love—and therefore, they're all gateways to creative artistry. In this first section of the book, I'm going to show you what that means for you and how to find the artist of love waiting to jump out from inside your lovely feminine self.

THE ARTIST

In my late twenties, I started training, auditioning, and working as an actor. I learned how to create an entire backstory for a character out of a ten-page script. And then I learned how to act the role of that character—how to demonstrate sadness through my eyes, how to show longing through my body, how to reveal distrust through a sidelong glance, how to embody crazy, kooky, fun, loud, bitchy, playful, annoying, jealous or mean. I learned to play a slutty best friend, a popular girl with hidden insecurities, a dumb bimbo who gets murdered in a dark basement, a hard-driving reporter, a twitching crystal meth addict, and so many more.

And playing all these roles led me to discover more of myself. It was liberating and energizing to feel how being slutty or ditzy or addicted would move through my body, and then reveal that newly-discovered part of myself to a live audience of witnesses.

I loved acting—I still do!—and for a few years I found some decent success and fulfillment as a working actor. But it wasn't until I began applying acting, theater and storytelling to love itself that I began to watch my entire life change, leading to more sex, magic, color, emotion, expression, peace and creativity.

A first date was no longer a first date—it was an audition, and I got to decide which costume to wear, how to act and what my main flavor of energy would be. A fight was no longer just a fight—it was a necessary conflict between two characters that needed to happen so the plot could move forward. Sex was no longer just sex—it was a scene that needed to be set with the perfect lighting, sound and design.

And above all, I was not just Madelyn. I was an actor of life and love who had thousands of parts to play, costumes to wear, and emotions to embody. All of life became a magical stage, empty and ready to be filled with whoever I decided to be. This liberating revelation has led me to better sex, longer-lasting love (with myself and with others), constantly-flowing creativity, and a deeply intimate connection with my divine feminine nature. All because I gave a voice to the thousands of different versions within my one body.

This is what being an artist of love means. Just like an actor who is trained to play all types of characters, you are capable of being all the things a woman could possibly be: the all-seeing oracle, the sorceress, the shy librarian, the devotee, the brat, the healer, the inner child, the maiden, mother, crone, the priestess, the queen, the wild woman, the witch, the medicine woman, the enchantress, the tantrika, the pre-teen, the wolf woman, the bitch, the boss, the sacred slut, and everything else in between.

And by becoming an artist of love you will inherently know how to summon these different parts of your unlimited self, whenever and however you desire.

You will have the tools to summon your inner oracle whenever your beloved is in need of some sage advice. You will have the tools to summon your inner queen whenever you are being treated poorly and need to walk away. You will have the tools to summon your inner priestess whenever your relationship is drying up and you want to have an erotic evening with sexual rituals and delicious ceremony. You will know how to summon your inner healer whenever you are lost in a deep ocean of grief and need to set boundaries in order to take care of yourself (even if it means also summoning some of your inner bitch to ward off unwanted advances).

And you will no longer be consumed with the fear that your man is going to leave you for another, more exciting woman.

You are already *all the women in one.*

There is *nothing* someone has that you do not have. You are everything.

THE ART

Art doesn't have to be acting. It can be anything you make with intention — a pouty face, a tantric ceremony, a comedic skit, a dance of longing, a dominatrix experiment, a self-directed short film, a honest expression, an embodiment practice, an open-hearted temper tantrum, a self-portrait session, exquisite hair braiding, role-playing as a Sacredly Submissive Housewife, a ceremonial spanking, elaborate costume makeup, a flash mob in a mall, a specialty playlist, a song sung down a grocery aisle, a piece of kintsugi pottery, a portrait made with papier-mâché or a care package you send to a struggling partner.

Art is anything you do to open the moment to more love — with or without a partner, a witness or an audience. Art, even when shared with the world, is *always* firstly about you doing it for you.

Being an artist of love can look a whole lot of different ways.

For some of you, it may always be about making something with your hands—like pottery, painting or sculpting. To work through a breakup, you would best move through your grief by making a huge vision board to hang in your reading room. Or if you're in a relationship, when things get stale you're likely to lay down a tarp in the garage and create an intimate body painting date to connect more intimately. Or if you want to create something not just for yourself or your beloved, but rather the *world*, you decide to hold a pop-up art show and display all of your work over the past several years to celebrate with friends and family (and make some money!).

For others, it may be something you do with your literal body, like singing, acting or simply expressing in any given moment. During a breakup, you may become an artist of love by lighting your entire living room with candles and dancing throughout the space for yourself. In a relationship, you may send erotic videos to your beloved to spice things up while he's on a business trip. If you want to go beyond just yourself and your partnership, you may go to an open mic night where you perform your latest song or work-in-progress standup comedy skit!

Art can even be a moment in time—like stomping your foot when you don't like something rather than mechanically, professionally saying, "I do not like that."

Art can be an *expression!* An unfiltered reaction! A *revealing* of your heart, rather than a speaking of it.

Sure you can always speak your mind, by saying something clearly and cleanly like "I do not like that." But what about *also* trying to use your body language to reveal something?

Women have been shaped into so many different boxes for so long that many of us have lost connection with our bodies, including our body's *reactions*. After years of hiding our reactions, out of fear they will be too much, too big, too insulting, too ugly, we have muted our own sensitivity and therefore, the ability to respond to life in the moment. Most women have to wait hours and hours, if not days or weeks, to actually know how they felt about something.

Art is about *opening* those channels again. Being an artist of love means being impulsive as well as improvisational. Your art can be something carefully crafted with love, as well as something spontaneously given without a care in the world or any unnecessary premeditation.

THE THREAD BETWEEN
CREATIVITY AND LOVE

I n the Western hemisphere, particularly, it's much more socially acceptable for a woman to wait and receive rather than it is for her to create and initiate — and it's even more prominent in other cultures. You have been designed this way.

It's more appropriate to be *chosen* than it is to choose, to be *desired* than it is to desire, and to "*call in*" than it is to create.

Being creative in love is to claim what you desire and then incarnate *as that desire.* If you want to cultivate chemistry with your partner, you become She Who Craves Deeper Sex With Her Beloved in everything you do: from how you dress, to how you eat, to how you speak, to how you breathe, to how you make love. *What* you do doesn't matter so much as *how* you do it. Your desire becomes a daily practice, just like showing up to your yoga mat.

Let's not mix up the idea of being *creative* with being *aggressive.* Aggression is about forcing your way through with fiery action. For example: making it a prerogative to always make the first move or to go after what you want with fervor would be aggressive. Aggression is more about what you do, than how you do it.

An aggressive approach to finding love is to orient your whole life towards getting the thing you want: signing up for speed dating every week, flying across the country for singles' events, asking out as many men as possible, writing lists of your dream partner from their height to their job, signing up for matchmaking services, etc.

There's nothing wrong with this approach—it's just not the approach I'm speaking about.

What I'm talking about is the idea that you put more emphasis on who you are becoming than on what you are getting. Being creative in love is about *becoming*, not just finding.

Here's why: many women think that once they finally get the thing they want, they'll be happy. If they find the man of their dreams, they'll finally feel like a goddess. If they get married, they'll finally feel secure. If they get respect from the world, they'll respect themselves.

But it never works this way—not until you make the full-bodied decision to become, and create, the thing you want. To feel like a goddess, you must treat yourself like a goddess. To feel secure, you must create security. To feel respected, you must respect yourself.

While your life may inherently get better by deepening your partnership or falling in love, your deepest craving will only be satiated in the process of *becoming* what it is you want.

The marvelous thing is that relationships actually give you even *more* of a reason to discover your range as a woman. Not to please your man or become someone else you're not, but to discover more of yourself. And the more you discover of yourself, the more energy is available within you—energy needed for yummier, juicier, sex. Your sex life sucks because there's no energy flowing into it! Infuse lifeforce into your own feminine heart, and automatically you'll have more passion, excitement and aliveness to bring into the bedroom.

In order for the sex to go deeper and the relationship to last longer, you must prioritize the quality of your love before the quantity. Most people are just trying to make it to forever together, so much to the point that they stop actively choosing each other. Instead of doing the work to create a fruitful, engaging partnership, they fall into routine, forgetting about why they even fell in love in the first place. They grow bored.

The best, most enchanting relationships are born in partnerships where both people actively chose themselves, and chose their partner… every, single day. It's a daily choice. *I choose myself. I choose you. I choose us.*

Because this kind of relationship is an active, daily choice that requires active, daily effort. This flavor of partnership will require you to sacrifice your ego, be uncomfortable, take responsibility, open your heart, be creative, make an effort, and endure some sticky, confusing growing pains. And while some of that may sound daunting, it's daunting only because it will require you to really show up.

Since we live in a fast-moving society where a two-minute video feels too long, where two-day delivery isn't even quick enough, and where our groceries can be delivered within a matter of 30 minutes, it's no surprise that creating depth and staying power in a partnership is a challenge. But learning tools to both stay in a relationship *and* deepen it simultaneously is why you're here, and that's what you're going to learn.

The love story is not about how you met—it's about everything that happens *after* that fruitful day. It's about who you become in the name of love.

FEMININE AND
MASCULINE POLARITY

A key aspect to becoming an artist of love is having an array of tools.

One artist may prefer to tell her story dancing with a pair of polished ballet shoes, but she may also love to collect an entire studio's worth of paintbrushes for weekend painting.

Another artist may have three different types of guitars she likes to play when performing live, but spends a typical Saturday afternoon recording new jams for her personal channel on a digital keyboard.

An artist doesn't usually have one form of creativity — they have many. If they only stick to one method of creativity, day in and day out, their art starts to suffer. There's no room for new insight to mysteriously enter through a backdoor or two. There must be diversity in order for creativity to flow!

(This is, perhaps unsurprisingly, why this book is going to talk about so many different ways to be an artist of love — all of which are valid, workable, and powerful.)

When it comes to the artistry of *love*, feminine and masculine polarity is one of the key tools in your creative box.

Feminine and masculine energetics, otherwise called "polarity," is a natural law of opposition. This is based on Indian Tantric philosophy, where the feminine is referred to as "Shakti" and the masculine is referred to as "Shiva."

Shakti is the female principle of energy, which is our rightful definition of the true blue feminine. The feminine is not merely receptiveness (though she can certainly receive) — she is *energy*. She's the erotic energy that ripples up your spine in an orgasm, the electrical current that runs through cable lines and the color moving across your television screen. Shakti is the representation of the great feminine energy in all of life, nature, the elements and in humans.

Shiva, the representation of the masculine, is a well-known male deity in Indian culture, known as the god of destruction. Destruction, though, means something more along the lines of *He Who Destroys Anything That Is In The Way of Light and Love* rather than *He Who Throws a Fist into the Wall*. Shiva is loving but fierce; he is a good, gracious god who loves fiercely and will protect his devotees into battle. Shiva is deep as fuck, and spends more time resting in stillness than he does bustling around trying to get things done. This is what the masculine really is — deep, devotional presence.

THE MASCULINE: CONSCIOUSNESS

The masculine is consciousness: it is the part within you that has never changed. Meaning, it's the part of you that's *always been* — since your past life, in this life and in your next life. It's unfazed by attitude, it's unchanged by preference, it's unmarked by needs and it's undeterred by discomfort.

The masculine, being consciousness, is like a vessel for magic to occur within. Rather than being the magic itself, the masculine is like a cauldron that holds the sacred brew. The masculine is the river bed that gives the water direction and form (and actually makes it a river, rather than a puddle). The masculine is the depth that gives our desires, energy, and emotion direction.

THE FEMININE: ENERGY

The feminine is energy: it's the part of you that is *always* changing. While the masculine is about depth, presence and direction (linear qualities), the feminine is about movement, flow and light (nonlinear qualities).

The feminine is everywhere in nature: she is the sweetness of a babbling brook and the raging unpredictability of a torrent, the sway of bamboo and the ferocity of a forest fire, the drip of morning dew and the wildness of a tsunami. Like all of nature, the feminine is nonlinear — there is no order or structure that she must follow. Once structure is added to chaos, you get something specific and harmonized (bank + water = river) but until then, you simply have flow, power, beauty and range. At her core, the feminine is the energy without structure.

POLARITY: CREATIVITY IN LOVE

Embodying these energies is a unique form of creativity. Learning how to fully embody one of these energies in any given moment will *polarize* your connection, meaning, it will put you and your lover into opposition (the good kind). This is what *creates* chemistry — a type of erotic friction that comes from opposition. This brilliant practice is a valuable tool in the sect of artistry I call *creativity in love*.

If you desire to embody the feminine, you become energy. Energy is transmitted through the body through movement, responsiveness, emotion, pleasure, pain and light. The feminine can look like swaying hips, a pouty face, a flip of the hair, dancing fingertips, an explosive orgasm, or even a fit of rage.

Anything that brings energy to an otherwise linear or straight-forward moment is bringing more *life* into the moment. Depending on what kind of energy you bring, you can determine whether that energy brings more love into the moment too.

If you desire to embody the masculine, you become depth. Depth moves through the body through grounding, stillness, breath, rootedness and direction. An embodied masculine being feels very different than a feminine being because they're *grounding*, not swaying. The breath becomes deep and full, the head becomes straight and sturdy, the feet become tethered to the earth. Whereas the feminine is full of movement, the masculine is full of penetrating presence.

So why do you need to know all of this if you want to be an artist of love? Because polarity is an artform. It is a paintbrush for an artist of love; especially if you want to feel the essence of love *regardless* of whether or not you're in a committed relationship. Feminine-masculine polarity is a dance happening within you as a woman, all on your own. By creating an intimate connection with this dynamic within *yourself*, outside the context of a man, you will better be able to do that dance with him when the moment arises.

A lot of what we're going to look at in this book, from acting practices, to emotional practices, to archetypal embodiment will be focused on *embodying the feminine*. All forms of energy are forms of the feminine, so anytime you deepen your emotional range, you are inherently creating more energy. These practices are here to bring more of you online — and it just so happens that simultaneously, you'll bring more polarity online too!

As an artist of love you have the opportunity to be *creative* in love using your various avenues of artistry. Creativity in love is the sacred act of turning water into wine, aka *life* into *art*. This can look like:

* Turning a boring old Tuesday where both of you would normally slide on your pajamas and watch three hours of Ozark (water) and instead, surprise your beloved with a candlelit ceremony in the bedroom, directing him to take a shower before entering your sacred temple (wine!).

* Turning a painful situation in your business, like being criticized, plagiarized or judged (water), into fruitful, supportive and juicy content for an upcoming video to help others learn from your experience (wine).

* Hearing something triggering from your partner and instead of crossing your arms and slamming the door (water) you choose to uncross your arms, make eye contact and softly show your beloved how their words hurt you through your tender eyes alone (wine!).

* Feeling old abandonment wounds come up as you become newly single (water), and decide to write an ironic screenplay about your life with an even more amplified, outrageous story plot. You get to rewrite your greatest victory, whether it's a drama, a romantic comedy or an outright horror film (wine).

* Feeling resentful because you're not getting the kind of appreciation you want from your partner, but instead of getting pissy or passive aggressive, you decide to film yourself dancing to an erotic song, peeling off layers of your clothing slowly while whispering, "I… want…your….love… *baby*" (wine, wine, wine!).

And no, you don't need a man or, even a modern day "Masculine King," in order to become a feminine woman with deeply devotional love to offer. That idea in itself is patriarchal and expired. You don't need a gatekeeper to access your creatively expressed heart. While much of this book will refer to things you can do in a relationship, you are the foundation of all relationships. The connection you have with yourself is where your artistry takes off.

You don't need *anything* outside of yourself in order to become creative in love. All you need is to feel the pulse of your heart, the blood of your womb and the strength of your legs, ready to bear down and birth some motherfucking art in the name of love.

THE ARTIST OF
LOVE ARCHETYPES

Not everybody loves to create in the same ways. To help you personify the unique ways you can become an artist of love, I've created four archetypes for you to study and embody the shit out of: the Loyal Oracle, the Playful Priestess, the Erotic Enchantress and the Sacred Devotee.

While these archetypes are going to be your allies in love, they are also going to support you in all realms of healing. They will help you reclaim fragmented pieces of your brilliance, leading to greater strength, boldness, self-love and internal knowing.

The great irony is, you will find a greater sense of *yourself* when becoming the archetypes. Every time you invoke their energy, you're choosing you because you're calling back a piece of you that you've neglected. When calling in their gifts, you are taking a stand for your own magic. These archetypes hold deep codes, my love. And they will support you FULLY in reclaiming what's rightfully yours if you invoke their energy with reverence and devotion.

In the following section, you will receive several essential pieces of information for each archetype, including:

* Golden Key: the main nugget you need to anchor into when embodying the essence of the archetype.

* Achilles' Heel: the biggest pain point/struggle for each archetype.

* Artistic Flavor: the main energy (*fuel*) each archetype uses as an artist.

* Creative Strategy: the specific thing the archetype does when she's creating art.

* Archetype Goddess: a deity or goddess that represents the archetype.

* Archetype Character: a character from television or film that represents the archetype.

Let's begin with the Loyal Oracle.

LOYAL ORACLE

Graceful – Intuitive – Wise – Dripping in Elegance

GOLDEN KEY: The Loyal Oracle is intuitive, sensitive and able to see the unseeable. She's the kind of partner who inspires her beloved to be better, every day. She demands the highest integrity, truth and love available in any given moment.

Once the Loyal Oracle has chosen a partner, she's deeply loyal. And not just to them — but to love itself.

That means, she's not afraid to speak about challenging topics or uncover deeper truths. She wants to get to the bottom of anything that's inhibiting the flow of love.

She will not settle for love crumbs! And her partner loves her for that. They can always count on her to unearth the truth, leading them both into deeper, richer love.

ACHILLES' HEEL: Because she's so sensitive, and so loyal, she has a deep capacity for feeling *all* the feelings. At times, this can feel like a major burden. Additionally, because she's so loyal, she may try to make a relationship that has run its course work past its expiration date, or to begin one when it's not the right time…and to feel the weight of making that relationship work landing squarely on her shoulders.

The Loyal Oracle must learn the sacred art of letting go, trusting that something better is on its way to her. She also must learn that even though she can see the future, she's not responsible for making it happen.

Without the proper support of women's groups, "me time," solo excursions, and play dates, she can get bogged down with the weight of being an oracle of love. It's important she surrounds herself with people, places and things that rejuvenate her and refill her emotional gas tank. It's also important for her to choose a masculine being who wants her intuition and knows how powerful it is. She will know when she is in this kind of relationship when she feels safe to explore a gut feeling, knowing it is safe to be shared.

ARTISTIC FLAVOR: The Loyal Oracle's fuel is her raw heart. In a world where most people tiptoe around an issue, get passive aggressive, explode/combust from pressure or just shove emotion right on down into the depths of their bodies, the Loyal Oracle shows us what it's like to simply feel it and reveal it. She doesn't overcomplicate her emotions or try to turn them into polished, rehearsed speeches. She simply shows the rawness of her heart in the moment.

For example, when her feelings are hurt, or something doesn't quite feel right, she may pull back her shoulders, lift up her head, allow tears to come to the surface of her eyes, and say one simple "ouch" as a way to reveal her feelings to her beloved. The texture of vulnerability, and going straight into the "heart" of all matters, is what makes her emotional depth impactful.

The same goes with her elation, frustration, fear, excitement, longing and all other emotions. She touches the heart of it, shares it and then lets the chips fall where they may. Because her emotion is so *real*, this kind of fuel serves both her and everyone in her life, beautifully.

CREATIVE STRATEGY: The Loyal Oracle's creative strategy is Gift Giving. Whether or not she's considered herself a good gift-giver in the past, she has a knack for giving beautiful, thoughtful presents.

Whether it's a hand-written note, a perfectly polished crystal, a Spotify playlist or a card left under her beloved's pillow, she gives her love through physical offerings.

The thing for her to remember is to slow down and be intentional with what she is creating, making or offering to those she loves. *What* she's giving doesn't matter nearly as much as the *how* and *why*.

ARCHETYPE GODDESS: *Themis.* The ancient Greek goddess of justice, Themis is often seen holding a sword in one hand and a scale in the other. The sword is a powerful tool that can slice through unconsciousness, lapses of integrity and injustice, whereas the scale represents the weighing of evidence. As an Oracle, Themis holds great power in keeping society flowing with equality, grace and morality. Her sage advice should be well-listened to, as she holds the key to deeper integrity for all.

ARCHETYPE CHARACTER: Arwen from *Lord of the Rings.* Arwen is the soulmate of Aragorn, the rightful King of Gondor. She is a radiant elven princess who has a gift to see into the future (she is literally an Oracle). In *Lord of the Rings: The Fellowship of the Ring,* Arwen gives Aragorn her sacred pendant as a gift to pledge her eternal love for him. When this necklace is given, it is a symbol that means she is willing to sacrifice her immortality in exchange to be with him, the mortal man whom she loves. She is a true Loyal Oracle.

PLAYFUL PRIESTESS
Youthful – Bright – Theatrical – Joyful

GOLDEN KEY: The Playful Priestess is a bright, colorful chandelier in any room. She's the embodiment of play, passion and joy! She's the kind of woman who reminds her partner why life is worth living. She loves picnics on the beach, splashing under waterfalls, wearing bright clothing that brings her joy, making funny TikToks, and seeing just how much she can play every day.

Her partner loves her playful spirit because it reminds him why life is so beautiful. She reminds nearly everyone to not take themselves too seriously and to simply drink the expensive champagne, wear the fancy outfits, book the spontaneous flights and spend the money on all the yummy things that bring pleasure! "Stop over-analyzing your joy and start surrendering to it!" she cheers.

Her spiritual practices may look different than others, so it's important she doesn't judge that to mean she's less evolved. While some people may do kundalini yoga and breathwork, the Playful Priestess may write a comedic play. While others may have formal therapy sessions, she may lean on improv classes. The Playful Priestess does the things that make her feel alive, uninhibited and free to express.

ACHILLES' HEEL: Though the Playful Priestess has a great capacity for joy, she can sometimes hide behind a rigid exterior. If her playfulness was shamed as a child, or she carries the "silly girl, stop that nonsense!" wound, she may have learned how to hide her playfulness behind a wall of to do's, practices, books, and scholarly pursuits.

Playful Priestesses who don't feel comfortable allowing their embodiment of joy to shine freely may rely on hyper-tight careers to keep them in check—anything with quick deadlines, fast-paced requirements, or controlling bosses. These careers feel "safe" because they are predictable and well-controlled. That said, they are *draining* to the vitality and vibrancy of a Playful Priestess. She's not here to be a marketing machine, or to hustle her way into love. Her only job is to surrender to the oceanic love that is always flowing through her.

The Playful Priestess may also clam up, or even become somewhat of an ice queen, during a fight, even though deep down she's desperate to make up and move on. As an act of love, her partner can help her break open her hard exterior by tussling, playing, or being silly with her. For example ... the Playful Priestess would respond better to a spontaneous wrestling match than she would to a serious sit-down conversation to work through her relationship disagreements.

ARTISTIC FLAVOR: The Playful Priestess's fuel is her playfulness. Underneath any rigid exterior or learned behaviors about "keeping a poker face" lies a true wealth of abundant joy, laughter and freedom. The more she can learn to play with this great cosmic drama, the more fulfilled she will feel as a woman, friend and lover.

For example, if her partner doesn't do the dishes, she loves to fall to the floor in agony and cry in a British accent, "I'm dying, my Lord! I cannot take another dirty dish!" She regularly whips out her special pair of sequined leg warmers to brighten tense, or boring, days. She enjoys making little TikTok videos with her own unique flare and sharing them for all the world to see. And she is most certainly the best friend to have when going through a break-up — she'll find all the ways to remind her friend why life is still worth living.

CREATIVE STRATEGY: The Playful Priestess's strategy is drama. While the word "drama" carries a lot of heat, drama is merely a genre — it's the amplification of life, emotions and the overall *story*. When actors come together to perform a *drama*, they must engage all of themselves. They must amplify their emotion so they audience feels what they feel. They must make everything bigger, deeper, and brighter! Drama for the Playful Priestess is, well, inherently playful.

The Playful Priestess is a pro at amplification. Her motto is "Commit to the theater!" and she will stop at nothing less than the brightest, most colorful, playful expression. The more permission she gives herself to take up space with how she dresses, talks, eats as well as with the roles she takes, the paths she chooses, the people she loves, the better life is for herself *and* for those around her.

ARCHETYPE GODDESS: *Lalita Tripura Sundari.* Lalita Tripura Sundari (not to be confused with Lolita) is a Hindu goddess who serves as the primary goddess of Sri Vidya, a sect of Hinduism that focuses on goddess worship. Lalita is often depicted as a 16-year-old girl, holding a sugar cane in her hand, representing vitality and growth. Even though that may sound young, she is referred to as the Divine Mother — the Ultimate Shakti who's given birth to the entire cosmos. Her name Lalita means *she who plays*, Tripura means *three worlds* (body, spirit, mind) and *Sundari* translates to beauty. She is the ultimate goddess of playfulness and beauty in this great wonder of life! She is also known for giving her devotees financial abundance and spiritual nirvana. She is a deeply powerful energy for any woman to invoke within.

ARCHETYPE CHARACTER: Lucy Ricardo from *I Love Lucy.* Everything the one and only charismatic Lucy does is infused with humor, playfulness and sovereign drama! She is a professional amplifier — using her body language, facial expressions, and tone of voice, she brings color, light and energy into every scene. One of the most entertaining things about *I Love Lucy* is seeing the many playful schemes, plots and tricks Lucy plays with her partner Ricky. In one particular episode, Lucy places a bet with Ricky that she can get into his nightclub even if he tries to keep her out. She makes three attempts, each one funnier than the one before, eventually sneaking all the way into the dancing chorus with Ricky laughing and passing over the money. It's always in good jest and playful spirits with Lucy, though she was equally a stand for her independence and can-do attitude. Take some time to study the embodiment of Lucy Ricardo to dive into the marvelous world of theatrical play.

EROTIC ENCHANTRESS

Shakti – Passionate – Sexually Sovereign – Ecstatic

GOLDEN KEY: The Erotic Enchantress's compass is her sexuality. She is led by what turns her on, sets her heart aflame, and sends pulsing pleasure through her body. Everything she needs to know comes straight from the cues of her own body.

The Erotic Enchantress enjoys foreplay with all of life. Nothing suits her more than leaning into anticipation, flirting with the great mystery and slowing things way down when she finds something juicy to sink into.

Sex is not just limited to the bedroom for her. Sex is something that happens all day long. It's not an event--it's a lifestyle.

That doesn't mean she's always *having* sex, but it does mean she's always connected to her pleasure. She loves adorning her body in lace, velvet and silk—she knows that not just *any* old fabric can touch her holy body. If anything is going to cover up her gorgeous, natural skin, it has to be worthy of being there.

The romantic partner of the Erotic Enchantress loves her because she unabashedly owns her power, pleasure and body. Though she may not always be *asking* for sex, her natural erotic nature is frequently sending out an invitation to her beloved, should they choose to make a move. And when they do — BAM! Spicy, sizzling fireworks abound.

ACHILLES' HEEL: Because she's dripping with eros, it can sometimes feel like she's never fully satiated. But alas, that's the epitome of the feminine — *period*. "She" is a never-ending bottomless pit of desire, love and intimacy. It's just a little more heightened for the Erotic Enchantress because her experience of longing is just as much physical as it is spiritual. She may fall into some frustrating sexual tendencies, such as projecting her desire for sex onto others, sleeping with people who don't fit her criteria for healthy partners just to get a quick fix, leading with her sexuality in order to get men's attention, or hiding her eroticism because she's afraid of its untrained power.

Learning solo, sexual intimacy practices for the Erotic Enchantress is just as important as brushing her teeth or exercising. Solo sexual practice such as neo-tantra, sacred self-pleasure, practicing with a yoni egg and giving herself embodied dance performances in the privacy of her own bedroom, ensure that she continues to create a healthy relationship with her eroticism.

For many women this is the hardest archetype to embody. Being an Erotic Enchantress may not come naturally at first--there may be a period of deconditioning from religion, society and culture to get to a space where she can even recognize that part of herself.

Instead of shaming herself for this, the Erotic Enchantress can use it as an invitation to feel her own longing even deeper. She can feel what's underneath the insatiable urge to unite with her lover — is it, perhaps, a longing to unite with the Divine? To return back to her original state of sacred union? To feel fully seen and met in love? Whatever it is, her self-exploration can lead her to accept herself as the Erotic Enchantress she is.

ARTISTIC FLAVOR: The Erotic Enchantress's fuel is her eroticism. When she's triggered, she best taps into her sexuality and then creates art from that place. Maybe she begs her partner to spank her for having an attitude, or she sends him an erotic video of her dancing in lingerie to Beyonce's song *Jealous* after getting into a fight about him talking to another woman. She might nibble on his ear and purr, "baby, listen to me," when he's not hearing her correctly (instead of yelling the same old "WHY DON'T YOU EVER LISTEN TO ME?").

To be clear, she never uses sexuality to manipulate a partner. She never gives the gift of her eroticism without connecting it to her heart, nor does she give it just to get something in return. Instead, she leads with her erotic nature as the way to bring more creativity to the moment and deepen the love that's already there.

CREATIVE STRATEGY: The Erotic Enchantress's strategy is dance. She *enchants* the world with the way she moves, like a dancer, through life. The undulation of her body, breath and emotions capture the attention of all around her—not because she *needs* it, but more so because *they* need it. In a world that is starved for intimacy and beauty, an Erotic Enchantress is a tall glass of water on a hot day. She quenches the thirst of the world with her sovereign essence.

Her dance doesn't always need to be sensual. She may dance to rock n' roll, rap or reggae, simply to feel the beat of something different. She can dance to convey messages to her beloved, or dance to please her own desires.

In fact, the Erotic Enchantress doesn't even have to be dancing in order to be "dancing." All of her life is a dance, moving to the flow of her essence: how she exercises, how she stands in line at the bank, how she walks, how she shops for groceries, how she goes to the post office and more. Her dance infuses every movement she makes, whether she's intentionally dancing or not.

ARCHETYPE GODDESS: *Isis.* Isis is one of the most prominent goddesses of Egypt, known for her gift of sexuality, fertility, healing and magic. She is the daughter of Geb, god of the earth as well as Nut, who is the goddess of the sky. She fell madly in love with her brother, Osiris, when they were only in the womb. And when Osiris was murdered, she was able to bring him back to life with her potent sexual energy, thus transcending even the darkest of life circumstances into something beautiful. She teaches that the art of sacred sexuality can be the most powerful of all.

ARCHETYPE CHARACTER: Samantha Jones from *Sex and the City.* Who could do the Erotic Enchantress justice better than Samantha? She is the perfect character for this archetype because she demonstrates what it looks like to be *fully sovereign* in one's sexuality. She is unafraid of basking in her right to receive pleasure however she wants. In the name of sex, she will cover hand-made sushi all over her naked body for her beloved to feast on, become temporarily lesbian, masturbate to her upstairs neighbor's loud sex, and welcome lovers into her apartment at 2 AM topless and ready to make sweet, sweet love. She enchants the world, her friends, and her lovers because of her unabashed love for sex, freedom and sensuality.

SACRED DEVOTEE
Tender – Spiritual – Mystical – Brave

GOLDEN KEY: The Sacred Devotee is connected to the thread of Spirit, and whatever that means to her, in everything she does. She is dripping in devotion to the gods and goddesses that she worships, and experiences ecstatic states of love when her devotion is enacted through ceremony, song, prayer and Temple arts.

Have you ever heard the phrase, "Everything she touches turns to gold?" The Sacred Devotee is like that, but with sacredness. Whatever she touches turns sacred, as she easily accesses the deeper meaning of life, especially in relationships.

When her heart breaks, she gives her grief to god/dess…

When she is longing, she makes her agony holy…

When she's in love, her body is in a state of worship…

This doesn't necessarily mean she's religious or has any kind of strict protocol for her spirituality, but she may find herself resonating with specific lineages of faith such as Tantra, the Kabbalah, Bhakti, Wicca, and/or Buddhism.

Spiritual practice resonates for her as more than just a thing she does, but as a lifestyle she adopts.

The Sacred Devotee's partner admires how devoted she is to love. He loves that she reads into all the angelic messages she picks up along the way and how she knows there's *always* a deeper message behind seemingly simple occurrences.

ACHILLES' HEEL: All of this said, because she's so devoted to love above all she can sometimes slip into the mindset of a martyr, particularly in the realm of wealth, security-building and structures. She will do wonderful things for the community such as volunteer for those less fortunate and donate to important causes, but either forget, or simply avoid, creating security for herself. The pendulum swings way into the feminine pole, and a little too out of balance from the masculine pole. This can be harmful to her relationships because she may outsource security to whomever her masculine partner is, hoping *they* will have the 401k, house, and comfortable dream life ready for her to walk into.

This can lead to a whole host of problems if it happens unconsciously. Her ambitions may take to the back seat, letting her partner's dreams be more important (since he's making the money). She may stay in toxic relationships past their due date because she avoided building her own bank account (I get it, why would you want to work when you can sing Hare Krishna all day?). She simply may lose sight of her own strength and ability to do hard things!

If a Sacred Devotee has her own business or dream, it's strongly advised that she infuses her same devotion to god/dess into the work she's meant to do. I encourage Sacred Devotees to charge what she's worth (and then double it). Money, spirituality, and ceremony all walk hand-in-hand for her. It's crucial for her to remember she is worthy of all the luxury in the world! Besides, the more money she makes, the more of a difference she can make. The wider her message reaches, the more she can impact. When she grows, the world grows.

ARTISTIC FLAVOR: The Sacred Devotee's fuel is devotion. She knows how to remain in devotion to the greater Spirit in all things—from washing pots and pans, to making love, to meeting a friend for coffee, to planting a garden and more. She knows that god/dess lives everywhere. One way that the Sacred Devotee really shines in relationships is that she can sense when the nervous systems of others start to get a little too activated or flighty, and will advise everyone to slow down, take space and come back together when you're all feeling more grounded. She's an emotional thermometer in that way. She is sensitive not only to tensions, but also with all other emotions. She loves to slow down and bask in the beauty of joy as if it's a delectable treat, soak in the emotion of elation as if it's a decadent dessert and feel the indulgence available in deep heartache. When connected to god/dess in all things, all things hold meaning, purpose and intention.

CREATIVE STRATEGY: The Sacred Devotee's strategy is ceremony. If she and her partner have gone through a challenging fight, she is the first to light candles, lay out the sheepskins and create a harmonious space to read freshly-written vows together. She is quick to play Gregorian chants in a bedroom that's hungry for angelic love. She is highly attuned to fabrics, scents, textures, sounds and scents. It's important for her to work on priestess arts such as tantra and dance, while also deepening her repertoire of ceremonies. The Sacred Devotee should trust her instinct when it comes to *creating her own* ceremonies for each and every occasion, rather than always learning ceremonies from others. She was born for this.

ARCHETYPE GODDESS: *Mary Magdalene.* Mary Magdalene was the devotional partner to Jesus—not the prostitute that she was rewritten to be. Mary Magdalene, a High Priestess, performed ancient rituals and anointings on Jesus to prepare him for the magnificent weight he was meant to bear; more so, they were divine, sacred partners. Jesus was fully man, and fully human—and fully in love with her. They were deeply devotional beings both *to each other* and *to god/dess.* Mary Magdalene is also known as the Apostle to the Apostles because of her unyielding faith, leadership and depth.

ARCHETYPE CHARACTER: Pocahontas. While the 1995 Disney film is an animated movie that has been majorly fictionalized from the *real* story of Pocahontas, the film demonstrates the way full-bodied spirituality can live within a woman who is devoted to the sacred above all. The character of Pocahontas has a deep connection and reverence to nature, and all beings, while listening to the inner callings and knowings of her heart. When remembering the scene with the famous song, *Colors of the Wind,* one can recall the beautiful offering Pocahontas was giving John Smith, teaching him about the sacredness of land, animals, and nature, and the inter-connected mutual relationship between human and world. She opened her heart to John when she looked past their differences and shared her world with him in this way. Pocahontas blends the worlds of nature, humanity and spirituality in a beautifully sacred way. (I also recommend you take the time to read about the true story of Pocahontas's kidnapping and tragic ending in respect to her real-life journey).

Artist of Love Archetype	LOYAL ORACLE	PLAYFUL PRIESTESS	EROTIC ENCHANTRESS	SACRED DEVOTEE
DESCRIPTIVE WORDS	Graceful, Intuitive, Wise, Dripping in Elegance	Youthful, Bright, Theatrical, Joyful	Shakti, Passion, Sexually Sovereign, Ecstatic	Tender, Spiritual, Mystical, Brave
GOLDEN KEY	She demands the highest integrity, truth and love available in any moment. Deeply loyal to both her partner and love itself.	She is the embodiment of play, passion and joy. She's always reminding the world why life is one big party.	She is led by what turns her on, sets her heart aflame, and sends pulsing pleasure through her body. Everything she needs to know comes straight from the cues of her own body.	She is connected to god/dess in everything she does; dripping in devotion, she lives her entire life as a spiritual practice. Everything she touches turns sacred.
ACHILLES' HEEL	Can tend to get lost in the land of feeling, and will feel burdened by the weight of the world. Might stay in relationships past their expiration date.	Can hide behind a rigid exterior if she feels shame or embarrassment in her playful energy. Will choose careers that require her to over-discipline herself.	Can sometimes feel like she is never fully satiated, and may feel shame for her bottomless pit of desire. Tends to oscillate between over-indulging and repressing her sexuality.	Can struggle to create security for herself, outsourcing it to partners who appear "stronger" than her. May develop co-dependency behaviors and forget to tend to her own self-sufficiency as a form of self-love.
ARTISTIC FLAVOR	Raw Heart	Playfulness	Eroticism	Devotion
CREATIVE STRATEGY	Gift Giving	Sacred Drama	Dance	Ceremony
GODDESS	Themis	Lalita Tripura Sundari	Isis	Mary Magdalene
CHARACTER	Arwen	Lucy Ricardo	Samantha Jones	Pocahontas

INVOKING HER
CREATIVE STRATEGY

You've now learned that each archetype has her own strategy for being an artist of love. The Loyal Oracle gives gifts, the Sacred Devotee creates ceremony, the Playful Priestess embodies drama and the Erotic Enchantress offers dance. And while these four forms of creative expression are specific, they are also endless. Infinite. Interpretable.

What *kind* of gift does the Loyal Oracle want to offer? A pottery painting class? A piece of pottery itself? A video of her teasing herself? A little rock she found on her first date with her beloved that she paints a mural on? A song she created by herself, creatively stringing together all the instruments in Garageband?

What *kind* of ceremony does the Sacred Devotee create? A candlelit love-making ceremony? A rose-petal-filled bath? A plant ceremony with sage, crystal, the perfect journeying music and a room filled with cozy pillows and blankets? A sacred oil-making ceremony with a group of her closest friends, creating blessed concoctions to present to her beloved?

What *kind* of drama will the Playful Priestess create? Will she gather her friends for a magical evening of sacred theater and performances? Will she write a screenplay about meeting her beloved for the first time and their unfolding love-story? Will she become a master of using her body as an instrument and allow the drama to pass through moment-to-moment through expression and honest reactions?

What *kind* of dancing will the Erotic Enchantress offer? Will it be a high-quality erotic video filmed with thousands of dollars of equipment in a studio she rents out just for this special gift, or maybe something shot simply on her phone in her own bedroom? Will it be a dance of devotion she spontaneously gives to her beloved in the bedroom (wearing her favorite adornments) on a regular Tuesday night? Will her dance be choreographed and taught to her by an ancient sacred dance lineage?

While there are thousands of ways to create art, we usually all have a few methods we resonate the most with. For me, it's acting (which includes sacred theater and video-making) as well as ceremony. What's inside those videos can range from a full-blown temper tantrum, to a sacred dance of longing, to a ten-second video of me sensually eating a blackberry (#berryporn). I consider most of my video-making to be in the *acting* category of art because in order to make the video land the way I want, I have to play full out.

Let's take a closer look at each archetype's **artistic flavor:** eroticism, playfulness, raw heart and devotion. These flavors are the fuels each artist creates *with*, and the creative strategies for each archetype as the mediums they create *through*.

I'm going to specifically speak to how each archetype creates out of her pain, or the more happenin' term these days, out of a *trigger*. A "trigger" is something that happens when someone gets their feelings hurt, feels offended, gets reactive or has any kind of frustrated response to an event, person or circumstance.

Because this world can be so damn traumatic all the time, it's common for people to have triggers daily: somebody comments something spiteful on your latest social media post, your partner doesn't like the dinner you made, your mom called to tell you that you look tired, your friend didn't respond to your text even though you *know* they have their phone, your Tinder date mocked your career, and so on.

The more connected our world has become via technology, the more opportunities people have to get up in your face, be in your space and pull up a chair in your mind. It's not like it used to be, even a couple decades ago, where the only way you could get a hold of people was to write, call or travel to them. We now have *instant* access to each other.

Humans need ancient outlets for these modern, hyper-active times. We need old, earthly, grounded practices to help us get back in touch with our own bodies. What is an older outlet than *creation*?

Creation is the original cure for loneliness! Genesis 1:1 states: "In the Beginning, God created the heaven and the earth." While I'm not Christian, I can absolutely get down with ancient texts and some beautiful words when I hear them. God/dess was alone, so He/She created life. Woman creates life. Nature creates life. Creation is the stuff we are made from.

By learning how to be creative in life and love, you're finding a way to actually *use* all of the otherwise inconvenient happenstances of this modern world in a way that alchemizes it.

You won't be carrying around age old resentments anymore — you'll be setting them free. You won't be spiraling about that thing someone said earlier, or bashfully hiding yourself back from sharing something in your heart, you'll be claiming it and artfully sharing it with love.

When you hide your truth, you hide your heart — and this the opposite of intimacy. When you withhold something that hurt you, you're essentially robbing the other person of the opportunity to support you in that feeling. Every time you willingly reveal something that hurt you, on the other hand, you are parting the Red Sea of Truth! You are making way for love to flow again, because you're making way for honesty to exist.

The thing that's so beautiful about being creative with your triggers is that you're able to find a way to both reveal *and* do it in a way that's without blame to the other person. Art is an expression of self, not a sentence put on someone's head. It's not "you are a bad person because you hurt my feelings!" it's, "Oof, I'm hurt. Please see me baby."

This kind of lifestyle will lead to everyone around you feeling safer to be themselves because they can trust you to bring forth anything that's not feeling good. And the more that people trust you, the deeper intimacy you can experience together—especially in relationship. Not to mention, the safer you feel in your *own* body, too.

TURNING TRIGGERS
INTO ART – EROTICISM

Eroticism is the artistic flavor you use whenever your *sexual* energy is intentionally involved. When you add sex energy to your art, you can *instantly* turn a trigger into a sexual gift. And usually, the deeper the shame you hold around the trigger, the deeper the sexual gift can be.

Here's a personal example of how I've used eroticism in my relationships to express and alchemize jealousy, rather than letting it sit there in my gut, swelling and blocking the flow of love.

A former beloved was hanging out with a large group of women for a company outing. He, a couple of men and a *whole lot of women* went to a swimming hole so they could "practice becoming one with the waterfall" or something like that. When I asked him how the day went, he said, "It was sweet. So much siren energy."

In case you don't know this, sirens are basically mermaids — beautiful, seductive water nymphs whose songs lure sailors to them.

So naturally, I was all, *"EXCUSE ME, SIR, BUT ARE YOU CALLING THESE WOMEN MERMAIDS BECAUSE I'M THE ONLY GODDAMN MERMAID YOU'RE ALLOWED TO REFER TO."*

In reality, I first told him in a very straight-forward manner that his comment hurt my feelings because I hadn't seen him in a few days and I was feeling sensitive. The thought of him swimming with a group of beautiful mermaids felt like a big ouch, even if he said absolutely nothing insensitive.

He apologized, and empathetically said he could totally understand why that would not feel good. But while I really appreciated his response, I wasn't done yet. I needed to create. I *had* to create. I was bursting with a desire to create!

(Remember, merely getting the thing we think we want — like an apology — doesn't give us the thing we *really* want. What we want in these scenarios usually has little to do with getting, and mostly to do with *creating*.)

Once evening came, and there was very little light in my room, I lined the walls with candles. I grabbed my beautiful ceremonial dagger and took a photo of myself holding it in a very seductive way, with only my outline and the pointy dagger's edge clearly showing. I texted the photo to him with the words, "This is what I'm going to use on you and your little sirens." I filmed a video of myself dancing with the dagger as a cherry on top. And then I sent both the photo and the video to him.

If you're thinking that sounds, well, pretty dark...you're right. And I'm not saying the Erotic Enchantress is all about channeling dark emotions — trust me, she can be plenty bright and loving and cheerful, too. But when you're alchemizing a trigger through art, simply piling love and light onto the stickier, more painful emotions like jealousy or insecurity doesn't really free them up to the extent that they need to be truly resolved. In fact, sometimes it makes those emotions even more intense and prolonged.

Have you ever experienced something that caused you to feel pain, and the only thing you felt like you "could" do (if you wanted to be a good spiritual woman, that is) was to move forward was something uber calm, grounded, and mature — like meditation or journaling?

You sit, you breathe, and you wait for the spiraling, cycling thoughts to stop.

Sometimes this helps, and sometimes this makes the emotion even more intense and prolonged.

Debbie Ford, author of *The Dark Side of Light Chasers*, calls this the Beach Ball Effect: suppressing emotions in effort to be spiritual is like shoving a beach ball under water hoping it'll stay there. Eventually, it'll burst up through the water, nose-punching you in the process, and you'll have used up all your energy trying to hold it down.

When you create out of your pain, you are playing with your shadow in a way that is healing rather than harmful; you are taking initiative, rather than waiting to see what happens by luck or chance or hope. This is empowered, artistic shadow work—and you have every right to take up this flavor of space. In fact, the world is hungry for it.

Most people consider their darkness to be *so* taboo, *so* shameful and *so* unacceptable that they force it way down, deep into their psyche where cobwebs and dust accumulate, only making the beachball bigger and the pain point more sensitive. By expressing this energy in a creative way right from the beginning, you're validating yourself by taking up space and refusing to hide. YUM.

While this siren moment is just one example of using eroticism to create art when I was triggered, there are oh-so-many ways you can create art in the moment using your sex.

You can playfully dominate your partner while wearing red leather, slide a pair of panties in his work trip bag with a note saying, "Don't forget whose panties you make wet. I love you," ask him to pick up a ball-gag on his way home from work so he can use it on you next time you emasculate him in a fight, or write a steamy haiku about what you're going to do if he doesn't pound you into oblivion in make-up sex.

Remember, you're not manipulating him with sex nor are you being sexy because you're a woman and that's what you "should" do. You are liberating your own heart through eroticism — for yourself. It just so happens to open your partnership to deeper love, passion and excitement as well.

The most important thing is that you let your gift of eroticism come from the love you have *inside* your genitals. Fill your sex with up with so much heart that you penetrate open your own frustration and then share that liberation with the man you love.

TURNING TRIGGERS
INTO ART – PLAYFULNESS

Did you know that your neural pathways cannot experience humor and anxiety simultaneously? The Playful Priestess sure does.

This archetype in particular knows the transformative power of play above all. Sure, you can always immediately book a session with your talk therapist, write down your many thoughts in a journey, or contemplate the vast intricacies of your childhood trauma recreating themselves in your modern-day life… or you can HAVE FUN! Laugh. Play. Run into the big-bosomed embrace of mistress joy.

When I think about how the Playful Priestess creates art out of her triggers, I'm reminded of a Facebook post I saw a few years ago that continues to be one of my all-time favorite pieces of playful relational art. Like, ALL-TIME all-time. *That* good.

It all started with a dirty sock. Kestrel, a 10-year old girl, had a bad habit of leaving her dirty clothes around the house. Her mother, Xep, not wanting to pick up her clothes anymore, decided to make Kestrel's one lonely bathroom floor sock the star of an artistic experiment.

Xep created a white label with a black border (like the labels you see at museum exhibits) and turned the sock into an exhibit. The exhibit was titled, "The Forgotten Sock."

Instead of picking up her sock, Kestrel decided to play along with her mom and added more to the exhibit, like a small wooden altar and barnyard animals to "worship" the sock. Overtime, the scene became more and more elaborate as the two of them added more to the sock exhibit in a playful standoff.

This mother-daughter experiment went viral after being shared on Facebook. The Washington Post even wrote a story on it, which you can find by searching for, "How a Mother-Daughter Standoff over a Dirty Sock Became a Viral Sensation." I recommend you look for it so you can see photos of the final product!

I've never worked with Xep, but I can tell you she's definitely in touch with her Playful Priestess. She could easily have turned the sock into an argument with Kestrel or a chance to lay down the law, or even a reason to fold in on herself and question her capabilities as a mother. But instead she turned that trigger into an opportunity for art — and I guarantee that doing so strengthened her relationship with her daughter.

Is your partner misusing your favorite sautéing pan by covering it in the cheapest baking spray possible? Instead of snapping at him or forbidding him the use of the pan, try running around the house, holding the pan, dramatically yelling in agony, "Not my pan! Not my sweet, lovely, cherished, beautiful baby of a pan!!" until you fall to the floor, coughing and dying next to your beloved pan. This will get your point across…but it will also turn your trigger into an act of playfulness that your partner can engage with.

As you do this more and more, your partner will start to feel free to bring their own playfulness out in service of the relationship. One of my favorite film examples of this is in the movie *No Strings Attached,* where Adam (Ashton Kutcher) made Emma (Natalie Portman) a period playlist "to help soothe her womb." He added songs such as *Sunday Bloody Sunday, I've Got the World on a String, Bleeding Love* and *Red Red Wine* as an offering to her moon time. This was playful, yes, but so much more.

One important note on comedy: you can't determine how it lands for others. That would be an utterly impossible task. Can you imagine how annoying it would be if you went into an art museum and at each painting, you had the artist telling you *exactly* how you needed to feel when you looked at their piece? And that any other feeling is wrong or not allowed? Bleh. No.

Every time you bring creativity into your relationship, you are out of control of how it lands. Every time you put your love out there, you are out of control of how it is accepted. Every time you make art, you are out of control of how it is interpreted. And it's true — some of your playful efforts will fall flat. Your partner won't get them or won't laugh when you want them to or won't want to engage. *And that's okay.*

The point isn't to get a particular result from your partner. The point is to turn your trigger into art through playfulness. When you free yourself from the dead weight of having to control someone's experience, ultimately you will free yourself to keep making art. And the more art you make, the more your partner will feel free to engage with it.

TURNING TRIGGERS
INTO ART – RAW HEART

The heart is the compass of all art, no matter if it's raw, erotic, playful, or devotional. The heart is the North Star of your artistry, pumping life force into the creativity you birth. Everything is an extension from the heart, which is why it's so important to learn how to open it. Take it from the Loyal Oracle… she knows.

When I refer to the raw heart, I'm speaking specifically to the most tender of soft spots in your heart space — the ones generally protected by a fire-breathing dragon, a crocodile-infested moat, a magical circle of protective spears and an angry best friend.

Embodying "raw heart" means deciding you're going to strip away those tough barriers and expose your longing, grief, desire, fear, confusion, upset or whatever else is present in the name of love itself. But you don't just express it, you *incarnate* as it. You become the emotion. That is the art of the raw heart.

Raw heart artistry doesn't come with as many bells and whistles as the other archetypes. It can be quite subtle, in fact. This is the only artistic flavor that focuses less on invoking an energy, and more on being with what is right there, underneath the surface already. Whereas devotion, eroticism and playfulness need to be invoked, the raw heart is always current. The only thing you need to do is strip away the mask of stoicism and tough-girl swamp muck to reveal what's real for you in the moment.

Here's an example of a raw heart moment that was completely unexpected: I was in recovery mode after an argument with a lover. I was feeling particularly closed after a fight—I wasn't in the mood for any of his so-called "masculine leadership" and I was having a hard time opening through our discouraging dynamics to gain trust in him again.

He was using all of his tools: asking me to share my resentments, creating space for us to talk, giving me time to open at my own pace. Nothing was working.

After a while, he said, "Well…we could wrestle?"

My entire body gave a resounding yes. We got on top of the same sheepskins we usually made love on and had it out — he pinned me to the ground, I flipped him onto his back, he pulled my hair, I nibbled on his hand.

Right when he was about to dribble a taunting man-loogie on my face while he had me on my back, I felt my heart melt open. I started to cry. All of the pent-up closure I experienced opened and I went on a babbling rampage saying things like, "I don't know how to be in a relationship, I'm a failure, I'm scared, I love you!"

The wrestling itself was magical in its own way, but what came *after* was real magic: from the physical embodiment of our wrestling, I broke open and touched a much deeper truth that was living underneath my closure: "I don't know how to be in a relationship."

This statement isn't true…I know how to "do" relationships. And yet, this tender truth was coming from deep within my inner little one. The tiny girl in me who didn't feel safe to open her heart in her childhood because of the pain she experienced. *That* part was true.

In that particular relationship, I would sometimes feel stuck when it came to opening my heart after a fight because our fights were really painful. My inner child felt stuck on how to open when she was afraid, therefore, my raw heart artistry was to merely share that piece of me and let her be witnessed.

There was no performance. No theater. No skit. No dance. No emoji story-telling. No video making. Just an open, vulnerable heart and a rich opportunity for radical intimacy.

The act of revealing is based on what happens in the body, not in words. If you do want to say something, you can get across a lot more saying something simply, like, "Baby. Look at me. I love you. And this is how it feels to love you" rather than grabbing the pitchfork and listing off your go-to list of their wrong-doings in the last five years.

A key element to incarnating as a raw heart is to use your physical body as an instrument of expression— it can't *only* be internal emotion. Uncross your arms, soften your eyes, pull back your shoulders, and let it all be messy. Because let me tell ya—being seen in your tender feels, without any hiding or resistance, is going to feel messy!

Being that you're a living, breathing instrument, you can use your body to make sounds and reveal how you feel in more artistic ways. I once felt like my heart was on the chopping block because I loved a particular man so fucking much—the only way to describe it was that I felt like a constant sacrifice to love. I showed my partner what this felt like by extending my arms as wide as possible and throwing back my head. I let my chest heave up and down as tears fell down my face. Opening wider and wider, I fell into his embrace.

The more you open to the messiness of your heart, the more open the moment is going to feel. The more you try to control the messiness of your heart, the more rigid the moment is going to feel. Trying to control your heart is really counterintuitive to how the healing wants to happen, and yet, letting yourself be messy is wildly counterintuitive to most humans.

Let yourself feel all the questions as they arise. Will they still love me if they see this side of me? Will they leave me if they see me cry like this? Will I still be beautiful to them if they know how dark my pain can be? Will they pity me if they know how deep I can feel?

Use these questions to feel deeper! Let what arises be here. Let it pull up a chair and feel welcomed by you, rather than repressed and shamed.

As an artist of love, the most important thing is not revealing to your partner, it's the act of revealing to yourself. When you stay with *yourself* as a core emotion comes up, you are taking a stand for your own right to exist. And so long as you do that, sweet artist of love, you will find that life has an interesting way of making sure only those who can truly meet you there are in your life.

So the next time your partner is playing video games instead of ravishing you into the bedroom, try showing him your raw heart in the moment. Instead of snapping or nagging or giving him the silent treatment, *reveal* how it feels to be second to video games.

Soften your breath. Let your belly relax. Keep your hands by your side. And let whatever truthful emotion you're experiencing inside come through your eyes. No words, no judgment, just an offering of your truth. Show him, as an offering of love, how deeply you love him and *want* to trust him and be valued by him. Show *yourself* how you feel—meet *yourself* in your pain. Stay in that space of revealing your heart to him, and watch how he responds.

TURNING TRIGGERS
INTO ART – DEVOTION

The beautiful thing about devotion as an artistic flavor is that it continuously asks you to check in with what the moment needs, what *love* needs, what god/dess needs, above all. And whenever you discover what love is asking of you, you do it, and you do it full out.

You can't half ass devotion (it's literally impossible). It's like in acting: if you want a role…you can't *half ass* your expression. Not even close. In fact, you have to *amplify* it. You have to make it obvious, big and bright. You have to get to the heart of the feeling and transmit it as truthfully as you can so that the room itself feels you.

Whereas eroticism, humor and raw heart can all be incredibly spontaneous, devotion typically asks you to slow down in order to tune in. There's a texture of mysticism involved—it requires feeling *beyond* the literal moment and into the tendrils of the unseen. You have to feel what you feel, yes, but then you have to become wider than that. You have to feel what your partner is feeling, too. And then what love itself is feeling.

Yes, you may feel irritable, grumpy or stressed out of your mind—but can you feel into the future, in a time when you know you won't be? Can you help yourself get through this challenging time *now*, knowing you won't remain in this state forever?

Yes, you may be feeling angry or your partner is feeling angry—but what is *beyond* that anger? What is the deeper truth percolating underneath the pain? The thing not being said or expressed?

Yes, you may hate what you see happening in the world—but what is underneath that sacred rage? What is the wider, bigger answer you are being pointed towards? The change you want to become?

A key element to devotion as an artform is that you must train yourself to go beyond the present moment, trigger, upset and reactivity and feel *wider* than what you are saying you want. What you're saying you want (whether it's for yourself, from a partner, or something in the world) is important, yes, but usually it's not everything.

Let's look at a relationship example. A student of mine, Cari, was once fighting with her partner Jonathan about something very small and silly—why he hadn't taken out the trash yet. She said something pissy and he took it to heart and got defensive as a knee-jerk response.

If Cari was going to make a choice merely from her own feelings, she may have done something selfish like slam the door and leave the room. This is a surefire way to end the argument for the time being, but it doesn't end the pain. And it's not healthy for the relationship—it can create a break in trust and an anxious attachment style in Jonathan.

On the opposite end of the spectrum, she could choose to pause and have a sit-down chat with Jonathan right then and there about the disagreement that was happening between the two of them, breaking down the feelings of inadequacy he may have coming up and the resentment she was holding back, as clearly these things were building up and needed to be cleared.

But, like many people, Jonathan wasn't usually able to sit-down and unpack a fight when he was feeling defensive. If all he could see was red and all he felt was defensiveness, he wasn't going to want to hold hands and make eye contact with steady deep breaths.

Knowing this about Jonathan, Cari decided the answer was *not* to have a sit-down chat and to instead create an environment where they could both wildly express themselves. This would be in devotion to what the moment itself needed.

She went over to their sound system, plugged in her phone and started blasting Rage Against the Machine. She turned the volume on high, started jumping on her feet and raising her hands in the air as if she was pumping up a wrestling stadium. She ran over to Jonathan and playfully chest bumped him.

He was *not* having it. But Cari didn't drop the art. She kept going, punching pillows and giving the brattiest performance of a lifetime.

Even though her experiment wasn't working in regards to getting them both to join in, she kept expressing *past* what she actually wanted. Of course she didn't want to be singing and moving her body—she wanted to slam the door and make him feel guilty. But as an artist of love, she had made a vow with herself to open *through* her resentments and create art through conflict.

And, of course, Jonathan ended up coming over and willingly tussling with her. As Rage Against the Machine blasted on, they had an embodied duel, taking turns witnessing each other's temper tantrums and praising the shit out of each other for it. A long epic night of sex followed immediately after.

Sometimes, all we need to do is express ourselves and be witnessed. But it takes deep devotion to the moment itself to be able to put aside your own closure, wounding or triggers and do what love itself is asking of you.

It also takes *humility* because whatever art you may try may fall flat on its face.

You may feel completely embarrassed or foolish. Good! The more foolish you can feel as an artist of love, the deeper you will go as an artist. You *have* to be willing to fail and feel alone in moments, like any leader.

GOING FIRST

There's a video called *First Follower: Leadership Lessons from Dancing Guy* that dissects what is required in order to start a movement. To teach this profound lesson, the narrator takes a three- minute clip of a man dancing by himself at a festival and shows how this one man, willing to be a fool, started an entire movement.

In the beginning there was only the man, dancing on his own like a crazy person. After a few moments, another man bravely comes up and starts dancing alongside him! This second man's role is crucial: he is the *first follower* and publicly shows everyone else what it looks like to follow.

This second dancer is the one who essentially shifts the first dancing guy from being a "crazy solo dancing guy" to being someone worth dancing with. The original dancer publicly embraces him and starts to dance with him, showing companionship and a welcoming attitude.

The second dancer waves a friend over and a third person comes over—*ah, the second follower!* Now, instead of just a couple people dancing, there is a movement starting to form. Three people tips the scale over into an intentional group rather than a random happenstance. Eventually two more, three more, and ten more come over, eventually leading to perhaps a hundred people rushing over.

Before long, if you were at that festival and *didn't* jump into the dancing scene you would be the odd one out. It's a very similar experience to a standing ovation — at first it's just one or two people, but the more who stand up, the more you're inclined to do the same (or else you may be judged for not taking part in the ovation — not that being judged matters).

This is what is called "holding the pose" in artistry. You hold to what you're doing. You don't drop it the minute you feel embarrassed or like it "didn't work." You keep holding it, and perhaps go even deeper: dance even *more* wildly, sing even *more* loudly, act even *more* seductively, reveal even *more* passionately.

Why do this?

Because *this* is what leads to the depth you are craving in love.

If you're sick of coming home to your partner watching video games as a method of zoning out, you get to be the one to surprise the two of you with a completely new reality. One full of ceremony and artistry and care for each other's growth.

If you're sick of first dates being boring as all hell, *you* get to bring the spark and play. You get to dress, talk and act as the archetype you most deeply want to experience, regardless of who this fellow is and what he likes.

If you're bored out of your mind with the same old serious dialogues you have with your partner after every fight, *you* get to be the one to make full-bodied expression a part of the culture in your relationship.

You don't have to wait until it happens to you. You don't have to wait until you find the perfect man who will completely understand this lifestyle.

You get to have sovereignty and autonomy over how you love... *now*. You get to create ceremony, depth, better sex and deeper love simply because you're the one who wants it.

You get to create the kind of full-bodied moments you see on the TV screens. You get to play out your fantasies, theatrics and dreams.

And remember, what you actually do (express, dance, paint pottery, sing, create an experience) doesn't matter so long as you do it with gusto, amplification and of course, devotion.

THE ACTOR WITHIN

While the archetypes provide context for how you want to develop your skills as an artist of love, there is one practice that can be used for each one—and also *beyond* each one—to become the truly limitless, boxless creator you are.

This practice is…acting. Acting is a boxless world. A beautiful, bright boxless world that not only allows, but *invites* you to be everything.

Whether or not you realize it, you are already an actor. Every time you go to the store and the cashier asks you, "How are you?" and you say, "Good, and you?" even though you are absolutely, definitely not doing good, you are acting.

The entire concept of society is an acting craft. You were born and then raised to fit into a certain laundry list of do's and don'ts in order to fit into society. *Do* be polite. *Don't* be aggressive. *These* are appropriate times to laugh. *These are not* appropriate times to cry. *This* is how you handle anger. *This is not* how you express frustration. OoOoOoh, hello there boxy box.

While the rules of society have created needed structure in an otherwise chaotic world, they have also implanted dogma and rigidity. You have learned some acting tools, and some characters to play, from society—but not all. You were given a cage, not a toolbox. And now…we get to reverse that.

By learning how to become an actor of life, you take your power back in all realms. You now get to choose, every day, what kind of character you want to be and how this character dresses, speaks, walks, works and makes love. *You* get to choose—not mommy, not daddy, not your partner, not society. *You.*

By learning some simple acting methodology, you can embody your archetype to fully "play the part" or you can go beyond the archetype and play parts not even mentioned in detail in this book. Become the Mystical Muse, the Frivolous Fairy, the Victorious Viking, the Slithery Seductress, the Man-Eating Mommy, the Destructive Diva or anything else your imagination can conjure.

Either way, learning acting skills will free you. And you do not need to be a trained actor, or have any interest in auditioning for roles, to fully reap the benefits of acting practices.

WHAT DOES ACTING HAVE TO DO WITH LOVE AND SEX?

From a feminine-masculine polarity perspective, discovering and embodying range is what leads to deeper, more fulfilling love and sex. And when I say "range" I'm referring to the gloriously long, limitless spectrum of characters, archetypes, energies, textures and personalities that can come within a human being.

When your partner insinuates that they love a particular energy that you may think you don't currently have (like bitch, slut, dominatrix, maiden, or priestess), they are serving as your acting coach at that moment.

They're showing you an energy that holds deep potential to be experienced *through* you and *with* you (not instead of you). They're saying, "Hey, I love everything you are. I *also* know there is more...."

This isn't said to hurt you. This isn't because you're not incredible as you are right now. It's because there is always going to be a deeper layer, a deeper truth, a deeper expression. We can always go deeper.

Remember, the feminine is literally energy. And energy is always moving, always changing, always transforming. If you embrace the one in you who is limitless, widening your range of expression is a part of your feminine embodiment practice.

Additionally, if you feel triggered by your partner always wanting more or something different, recognize the part within you, too, that wants range. You want your partner's ferocity *and* their gentleness. You want their sexual hunger *and* their soft melty open heart. You want their lightness *and* their darkness.

You don't just want his adventure-hungry knight — you also want his dominion-holding king. You want his darkness *and* his tenderness. You want him to go into battle *and* also fall into your arms. You want his man *and* his boy. You want his warrior *and* his magician.

We all want range.

The desire for range is not a threat…it is an invitation to bring more of you online. This is what being creative in love really means. You're committed to bringing forward something brand new and different; you're making something out of nothing, artistically, playfully and relationally.

Creating emotional and expressive range as a human in love is a lot like method acting as an actor. Method acting is a kind of acting technique where the actor fully identifies with their character's inner world and emotions, feeling what their character is feeling. The pain you see on the big screen makes you cry because it's *real*. And you can feel it.

As an artist, outside of any partnership you may be in, it is your holy responsibility to create range as a woman. Not for a man, but for you. Because living a life only knowing one thing can be draining, exhausting and color-less. Even if you are already the cat's pajamas, don't you want to know what it's like to be even *more* amplified? More seductive? More open? More expressive? More creative? More emotive? More magical?

When you as the feminine deepen your capacity for range, it inherently deep-ens your partner's masculine capacity for consciousness. But before you can take it to them—you have to start with yourself.

THE THREE LAYERS

Every actor has three layers of their craft: with themselves, with other and with the world. For a movie star, these layers could more specifically look like:

1. With Themselves: rehearsing lines in their bedroom, walking in circles trying one million different ways to say, "No, Thomas! You *must* stay if you truly love me!"

2. With Other: arriving to set to film with their co-star. This is the intersection for actors to bring their lines, emotions, and expressions together to create something out of nothing.

3. With the World: the big reveal! The movie is blasted out in hundreds of theaters across the world. Time for TMZ to be lurking around every corner. Fan clubs galore.

Just like an actor has three incredibly unique and equally important layers for their craft, you as an artist of love have the same three layers: with your-self, with other and with the world.

In the following three sections of the book, we will dive into each one of these layers one at a time to understand what it takes to become a limitless, box-less, sexual, hungry, open and multi-dimensional artist of love who is *in love* with her own damn life.

Part Two

THE ARTISTRY OF LOVE WITH YOURSELF

YOUR GREATEST LOVER

It's easy to think that the best, or only, way to understand love is to experience it in partnership. But there's an unskippable prerequisite to finding love with a partner: finding it with yourself.

This might sound like the cliché of "you won't be able to love another person until you love yourself." That's because it kind of *is* that cliché…and clichés are clichés because of the truth in them.

Can you create love and artistry with a partner if you don't feel those things in yourself? Yes…but it's a lot harder.

Have you ever wanted to take your partner out to do something totally different, like get a pedicure and drink champagne, but felt too awkward about it to invite him? Or have you ever had an unconventional idea about how to move through a fight, like a naked handstand contest, but felt prematurely embarrassed for when he might say no? Have you ever wanted to eye gaze during sex, but felt too insecure to initiate because you didn't know whether *you* could even hold your gaze for that long?

Everything you do in your partnership is born out of your relationship with yourself. In fact, your romantic relationship is a manifestation of the deep work you've done to love yourself. What you see happen in your partnership is a reflection of what is happening in your internal world.

When you're utilizing your partnership as a playground for deep healing, and *creating* instead of waiting, it's because you've learned how to feel safe during creative expansion. When you love yourself, you know that even in risky moments you're worthy and safe.

By learning the artistry of love with yourself, you'll have the tools to ground yourself when things aren't going well with a partner. When you start to lose your own footing in life, feel co-dependent, lose sight of what *you* really want, or start to prioritize the desires of your partner over your own, you'll be able to come back to your own body, your own creation and your own healing, because you know there is already a foundation of love and artistry there.

Plus, yourself is the one person you're always going to be in relationship with. No matter if you're partnered, dating, or single, you are always an artist of love with yourself. It is an ongoing relationship just like a garden. It needs seeds, soil, water and sunlight to grow.

In this section we're going to focus on mastering the artistry of love with yourself so that you can create an irreversible, irresistible foundation for love.

BORN INTO A BOX

There's little as devastating to a woman as the soul-sucking process of becoming someone else's ideal over her own. The contorting of her heart, her bigness, her expression, her dreams, and her desires to fit the mold of what someone *else* wants leads to a flavor of hopelessness that very little can compare to.

When a woman is forced to pretzel herself into a box (and stay there), she has to use an incredible amount of energy to remain within the perimeters. Whether she was born into a box already set for her, she was slowly and insidiously indoctrinated into one, she married into it, or she unconsciously chose one herself—a box is still a box.

There's a reason we are buried inside of a box; it is where we go to die. Not to live.

There are cultural, religious, relational, spiritual, emotional, and physical boxes. *This* is how you need to dress as a daughter. *This* is how you need to act as a wife. *This* is how you need to eat as a lady. *This* is how you need to behave as a friend. *This* is how you need to look as a boss. Women are raised with this kind of messaging in every direction, from community to parents to partners and culture. But nothing compares to the messaging she sends herself.

The endless boxes a woman has to somehow fit into, all at the same time, causes her to become paralyzed. She loses her will to move forward. She can't access her creativity. Her body doesn't feel like her own. Her womb is just another unseen organ. She doesn't feel inspired to have sex.

These boxes aren't always clearly in front of her face: they can be invisible, dangerous expectations that are passed onto her from someone else's ideals of what it means to be a woman.

Close your knees but always be available for sex. Dry your tears but don't be too tough. Put your children above yourself but don't let yourself go. Let men lead but don't ignorantly trust them. Speak up for yourself but don't hurt people's feelings. Let your hair down, but don't be out of control. Express the truth of your heart but ensure it's respectful, soft and sweet. Take care of your financials and future, but don't be an anal retentive tightass for goodness' sake!

Due to this unnatural conflation of identity, a gray blanket of "blah" is suffocating her wherever she goes. She pulls out her crystal dildo wand only to mechanically fidget and fumble for that "orgasmic" sweet spot but feels nothing but a tired wrist. She wants to cry and shriek from the depths of her soul, but can't risk disturbing the neighbors surrounding each direction of her apartment. She yearns to tear through the veil of claustrophobic misogyny hidden in every world she dips her toe into, but instead collapses into herself.

Whether she's single or in a relationship, she's comparing herself to the other women she perceives as more open-hearted, beautiful and worthy of a fucking amazing man. She wants nothing more than to be in a healthy, robust, fulfilling relationship but can't break free from her own self-judgment long enough to find out she's already that very woman who is capable of opening her heart, embodying beauty and being deserving of a fucking amazing partner.

She tells herself she's not goddessy enough, her heart isn't "open" enough and that she's always going to be just one of the guys.

She's bored with her sex life, but too lazy to change it. She's insecure that her partner will leave her for another, fresher, more alive version — the 2.0 edition. She's painfully self-conscious when moving her body in unfamiliar ways. She can't move to the beat of her hips. She can't even *feel* her hips. She is ridden with self-blame for not being able to break through all of this self-sabotage.

And one day, probably not too far into her life, she doesn't recognize the woman in front of her. She doesn't see the fearless, bright and shiny being she was born as, but instead she sees a carbon copy of all the stories, judgements and messages she has picked up along the way. She sees a quiet, subtle, one-dimensional version of her true essence — and she doesn't like it.

This particular flavor of reality, the one where you don't feel free to be yourself because you've been poked and prodded since birth to become someone you're not, is something that only a woman can really understand. Women have been told how to behave since the beginning of time — from being considered property to witch-hunts to household abuse to slut-shaming to being wrongfully prosecuted and more.

While we live in a much different time, there is still residue from all of this deep-seated patriarchal living. As a result, many women are struggling to tune out the noise from the world to discover who they really want to be. They're struggling to feel the true definition of *the feminine.* They're just floating around—disembodied women trying to *be* it all, while somehow missing the *mark* on it all. The byproduct is a lackluster life with boring sex, boring dating options and boring dreams.

By trying to stay within the lines and play it safe, this kind of woman loses the vibrancy of her soul. She dims the volume of her voice. She loses the fire in her womb. Therefore her romantic relationships, quite frankly, are boring. They're boring because they are missing the true essence of *her*.

The inherent expectation that a woman needs to fit into multiple boxes all to make the people in her life feel comfortable is the modern-day witch-hunt, with the slogan *fit in or be burned*. But the "burning" from those around you, as searing as their judgment may be, doesn't compare to the judgment you inflict on yourself. Stepping outside of the lines and risking being self-ish, weird, crazy, emotional, bitchy, slutty or inconsiderate brings up all your worst fears about not being…well, *good*.

You want to know that you're good—that the stuff you're made up of is *good*, that your heart is *good* and that your intentions are *good*.

But society is not the place where that revelation gets to occur. And deep down, you know that looking to others—including a romantic partner—is not the answer. The only person that will ever be able to validate, recognize and honor all that you are is you. The only person that will ever be able to create the life of your dreams for you *is* you. And if you want to go deeper in your relationships and reach ecstatic states in love, you have to begin to train that squishy silent self-approval muscle one day at a time until you are blasting off glass ceilings with your artistry, expression and unabashed states of energy.

It's time to stop looking to society in order to receive some lukewarm valida-tion that won't satiate what you really want. You don't want a good life—you want a sublime one. You don't want good sex—you want transcendence. You don't want a good partnership—you want devotion.

Even though today I delight in a waterwheel of creativity, a rich connection to my sexuality and an intimate connection with the many wildly feminine versions of myself, I was not born nor raised this way. Far from it: I was one severely domesticated bitch.

Being raised in a suburb of Dallas, Texas with two incredibly complicated, Southern Baptist, Republican parents, I received the brunt end of generational anti-women, anti-emotion, anti-expression, anti-free spirit and anti-feminist beliefs.

There was a box already built for me at birth. To be a "Moon Girl" (as my parents called me) was:

* To make it my one job to make my mother happy every day.

* To say my morning prayers every morning and confess my sins each night.

* To dress modestly so that I do not tempt boys.

* To ask for forgiveness to the Lord Christ Our Savior so that I would be taken up to heaven if the rapture happened and not left behind.

* To be able to read my mother's mind so that I didn't fuck up her life by doing whatever thing she didn't want me to do (I'm paraphrasing).

* To abstain from sex until I was married.

* To never talk back, even softly or respectfully.

* To, above all, honor my parents.

I had many stories and ideas planted into my head from being a small girl. I was told I was ungrateful, I was selfish, I couldn't make friends, I had a chemical imbalance and that I was broken somehow. One on occasion, after being broken up with, I recall being told I deserved it. Unfortunately, the more I was shamed and poked and prodded, the more emotional I became. The more emotional I became, the more out of control I felt and *wrong* for that sense of being out of control.

Eventually, I learned how to fragment myself into multiple pieces. I would separate from my emotions the best I could and numb everything that didn't feel like a Moon Girl.

By high school, I retreated so far back into my body, I couldn't find myself. I couldn't *feel* myself. And I unconsciously started looking for something I could control that would help me channel my repressed anger, but in a box of my own choosing. I needed to find a way to deal with my emotions that didn't require me to completely disassociate from myself, but would also allow for me to fit the bill of a good, polite Moon Girl.

Therefore, I did what many girls do and internalized my emotions by leaning on an eating disorder to feel that sense of control. My eating disorder came in the form of becoming a food deprived, treadmill-addicted, protein-powder-chomping bodybuilder. This path served one purpose: to feel less like myself. Because as far as I knew, who I was wasn't good. I was something that needed to be fixed. And my lifestyle choices, even if they looked "healthy" on the outside, were a manifestation of that self-loathing.

All the shame I felt about who I was deep down, and how "outside of the lines" my colors truly were, became self-directed. I had no method of expelling my feelings safely — most forms of expression weren't allowed. If I showed signs of the anxiety I felt, it would be used against me as proof of my "chemical imbalance" and I felt deeply alone in how to move through my confusion.

Bodybuilding was a way for me to feel in control — and in some ways, it was a form of self-harm. The more intensity, harm, and starvation I put myself through, the more in control I felt about it. The more I could do something with my blocked storages of energy. And the best part for me was that nobody would be questioning me—I was doing a bodybuilding competition, *what could ever be wrong with that?!*

A TASTE OF PLEASURE

I quit the bodybuilding lifestyle around the age of 23 because of a legitimate act of intervention by god/dess. After several years of rollercoaster training, where I'd gain weight to bulk up and lose weight to compete, I had had enough. I threw away my competition heels, packed my car and moved to the mountains. There was a lot that went into the next few years, including eating disorder healing, therapy, and bathroom floor break-downs, but I was still an endurance freak and got through that too.

In my mid-twenties I stumbled upon a few spiritual teachers who showed me how to honor my energy—meaning, my emotions, my curves, my body, my sensuality and my innate pleasure. I finally had a way to move the energy through and translate it into something nourishing and supportive: *feminine* energy.

I learned to sway my hips and dance in pleasure. I learned to open my heart and reveal my grief shamelessly. I was able to loosen the corset on my feminine heart so she could once more return to that childlike state of feeling just for feeling's sake. I laughed and cried and laughed and cried. I *opened*.

I discovered my turn-on for quite possibly the first time. I was alive! Pulsing! Pleasure-filled! Hungry! Sparkly! Energetic! Rosy! Juicy!

I began to date high-quality, handsome men who were looking for their dreamy, gushy feminine counterpart. And these men really *could* hold my emotions. They *could* take me into some deep, rich sexual places. They *could* validate my emotions and even honor them as beautiful, attractive and radiant.

But there was also a dark side. I began to discover, on the other side of the coin, that all of a sudden, I was expected to *always* be radiantly open. To *always* be in devotion to his leadership. To *always* reveal my heart artfully, and never in a passive aggressive or sharp way. To *routinely* be lost in pleasure with a yoni egg and crystal dildo first thing in the morning. To never lead with a complaint and *always* lead with a desire.

I would find myself in situations where I would be shamed, once more, for not packaging myself correctly. Sometimes my heart didn't open fast enough or wide enough for my partner, or I wasn't showing my "real" emotion to its fullest. I was rushed. I was criticized for my pace if it was too slow. And the most alarming discovery I found was that there was an insidious re-packaging of the idea that one should always trust their man's leadership *above* their own.

I was in another goddamn box and it was maddening!

Because while all the deep, tantric sex I was having was wonderful, the joy faded as quickly as it came when the other parts of me were not allowed to exist.

I realized that any kind of sex that required me to leave behind a part of myself in order to make it "deep" was not deep sex at all. It's flaky, unreliable and temporary. It may be beautiful, but it's not the kind of everlasting, oceanic sex I was hungry for. *That* kind of sex requires a foundation of safety, where I know, deep in my bones, all of me is welcome.

Not just the maiden, but also the wild woman. Not just the submissive, but also the dominatrix. Not just the pigtail-swinging cheerleader, but also the wise woman. Not just the doe-eyed housewife but also the strong-as-an-ox woman who beats to her own drum. Not just the woman who has her desires, but also the woman who has her complaints. The woman who doesn't just follow, but also leads. The woman who gets to be a messy fucking human like everybody else.

The question I kept asking myself was, "Where is the pocket of the world that doesn't demand a woman to be one particular way? Where there are no boxes she must pack herself into? Where everyone lays off, and lets her be whoever she is going to be and removes all their projections of who *they* think she should be?"

The answer, I found, wasn't anywhere I could move to. It was, in fact, only in the space I myself took up. That world was right there—in myself. And guess what? It's right there in *yourself*, too.

WHY YOU ARE
THE WAY YOU ARE

This is going to *blow* your mind: as adults, we either unconsciously or consciously set our lives up to try to get the exact thing we never received in our childhood. It could be physical safety, emotional wellbeing, stability or unconditional love… regardless of what it is, our *entire* lives can be spent in pursuit of chasing that one thing. Often we won't be able to get it, ironically, because we want it so badly that the very energy of wanting it repels it. Other times we will get it, but then push it away ourselves because our nervous systems don't yet know how to hold it.

I wanted to feel emotional safety—and I set up my life to get that very thing, whether in my bodybuilding days or the rosy-pink polarity world. The kicker was, in both scenarios I was looking outside of myself—to competition judges and "masculine" open-hearted men—for that safety, which is ironically unsafe. I didn't realize this until my late twenties when I started taking a good long gander at my proclivity for intensity, change, and control. I *thought* I was making life safer by feeling fewer emotions, numbing out and white-knuckling through any and all issues, but in fact I was making life less safe. I was further resisting myself, leading to feelings of self-abandonment. *Not safe.*

By holding my breath, sucking in my belly and being a self-contained good girl, my nervous system was always on edge. The good girl wound ran so deep it was sucking the life force out of all the inherent wildness that *is* the feminine. She wants to be open, messy, free and uncontrollable. And not always in a "dance by the fire and howl at the moon" glamorously spiritual kind of way, but sometimes simply not knowing what to do. Feeling lost. Being helpless. Letting go because you know it's okay to not have the answers sometimes.

I am certain that the reason I found myself in the hyper, driven, uptight, anal-retentive world of bodybuilding was because I was restricting my capacity to feel thanks to all the childhood programming I received around emotions and "crazy, bitchy, improper" women. And I am just as certain that I found myself in the enlightened tantric sex world because I was trying to turn that formerly-restricted capacity on just enough to make up for its years-long lack and get feeling "right."

Without fully knowing, I was convincing myself that if I could just eat less and work out more, I would finally be able to tolerate myself. Or if I could just learn how to reveal my heart in a "feminine" way, then I could finally learn how to feel my feelings in a manner that was perfectly, totally and completely correct.

Either way, I was concerned about avoiding all the icky, uncontrollable feelings that I made mean something about myself. I didn't want to feel my own pathetic longing for love, my own desperation for a partner who sticks around, my own deep fears around dying alone. If I could make all of that go away by focusing on dieting or becoming a mail-order goddess, by god that was what I was going to do.

When I finally realized all of my unconscious attempts for safety in these various ways, I was discouraged. It felt like I had more hard work to do and a lot of it—but over time I came to soften into the realization and eventually came to see it as a relief. If force was a part of my unhealthy pattern, then flow would be a part of my healing.

Flow would require me to listen to the deep yearning, the small whispers and the intuitive knowing I had within. It would mean it was time for me to choose *me* over any other teacher, leader, partner, mentor, parent, friend or critic. Choose me from head to toe: from who I am to who I am *not*, and to everything and anything in between. To not agree with everyone. To not "obey" anyone. To leave things when they are toxic or unhealthy to my inner little girl. To take a stand for my opinions rather than quietly disintegrate into the background. To feel emotions however I feel them without packaging them in such a way others feel comfortable.

I realized that for as long as I looked outside to others for the answers of who I need to be, I would remain in this unsafe pattern.

The way we exist in our bodies is the way we exist in the world. When I was a bodybuilder, my rigid body, diet, and mindset resulted in rigid sexuality, pleasure, and self-acceptance. Love needs a foundation of softness, malleability and flexibility. Not perfection, mind you, but devotion. Devotion to softening up even when times feel hard.

When I was abiding by the goddessy-feminine rules, I was no longer rigid but I was violently open. I was trying to open my heart as much as possible so that I was radiantly feminine, seductive and alive. I judged *all* rigidity and *all* closure, which continued to confirm to my nervous system that no matter what I couldn't trust myself. I was following another patriarchal protocol that was disconnected from the root of my own truth.

What I eventually discovered bypassed all blueprints laid before me: I realized that the only real need my nervous system had was to honor my truth. I had to stop listening to the ways the world says I should be and *honor what is*.

A safe body stems from an honest body. The more you put to the side all of the ways you're trying to live in order to be a specific kind of woman, the more your body can trust you to find your way.

CORE WOUNDS
AND CORE NEEDS

Before focusing too intensely on *who* you're attracting as a romantic partner, you need to focus on the *needs* you're attracting them to fill in the first place. As an artist of love, this is your golden ticket to the bullseye of your creative heart, and it will help you invoke deeper sovereignty in regards to the people you bring into your life.

I didn't start paying much attention to needs in a relationship (consciously, at least) until my late twenties. Until then, I was blissfully unaware of those unconscious patterns I was mentioning to you in the last chapter, and therefore dating anyone who matched up to the wounds I was projecting.

For example, during my bodybuilding days I dated other bodybuilders and intense meatheads who reinforced that laziness, flow and over-emotionality were all bad. I called in these partners because they were reinforcing my beliefs about "living outside the lines." They were all *super* intense, measured and controlled. I remember dating one guy who told me he would leave any partner who got fat because he doesn't respect laziness.

My need at that time was to be with someone who reaffirmed that life wasn't a playground to explore but a battlefield to fight. They were a match at that level.

During my flowy feminine days, I called in partners who reinforced the belief that the feminine partner needed to be an open-hearted goddess of love and light. They were all masculine-embodiment practitioners who took on the role of leadership, consciousness and depth, and desired their woman to live from her pussy and heart. And I love living from my pussy and heart, don't get me wrong. But I love it FOR ME. I love it because I choose it—not because it is chosen *for* me.

My need had flipped, and I was now attracting partners who demanded the opposite—all heart and no head. This led to gaslighting behavior from them on several occasions—for example, being told to trust him over me because it's ultimately the safest place for the feminine to be. Or being told that I'm "refusing his love" because I'm trusting my no over his request for a yes. This was deeply confusing behavior because *of course* I wanted to trust him, and I was left thinking, "Am I broken still? Am I broken because I'm not trusting you enough?" and things like that.

Both of these situations serve as examples for what can happen when you don't *choose* your needs consciously. If you're unconsciously needing negative beliefs to be reinforced, that is exactly what you will attract.

But if you take the time to sit down and choose the needs that are to your benefit and will contribute to your overall healing, you can begin to bring in partners who reaffirm who you *want to be* rather than what your wounded childhood nervous system thinks you need.

CLARA

Let's look at a different example to demonstrate the importance of *conscious* needs. My client Clara grew up in a family system that was unpredictable, chaotic and physically unsafe. Her father was an alcoholic who came and went out of their lives as he pleased, and her mother was in a new relationship with a new man every other month, creating a complete lack of stability and routine.

Her mother's partners would often dictate her mother's mood, because, like many feminine beings, her mother was on a search for the deepest love possible. But without having her own discipline and structure to separate her kids from her dating life, it always became one big mess. Clara's mother would spend a whole weekend crying in bed about the most recent guy who was a "big jackass" and broke her heart, all while neglecting to take Clara to her sleepovers or feeding her dinner. Clara grew up having to mother her own mother.

Clara's core need was stability—so she set her entire life up to receive just that. She got a decent banking job, she chose friends who had very little pizzazz so they were always easy to keep and she didn't take any risks when it came to adventure, finances and most choices. That said, when it came to love, her nervous system didn't know *how* to make a stable choice.

She went from lover to lover, consistently choosing men who were in need of "mommying" in some way: starving artists, emotionally frustrated military men and even several partners with terminal illnesses.

She needed to feel needed. In her body, *this* was what "stability" felt like because that was all she knew. As long as she took care of her metaphorical mother (meaning, whomever she was dating), then she would be able to keep them sane, available and in love with them.

The brain and nervous system register a romantic partner as your caretaker. This is why you end up re-living the same traumas you experienced as a child. Your brain says, "Okay, if I find someone who feels similar to the original caretaker who created the original wound, I can simply make them love me better this time and fix that original wound!"

Unfortunately, whomever you are dating is *also* human and is *also* putting you in the role of their caretaker. This is why relationships can create such deep turmoil and confusion—you are both trying to get your core wounds healed and core needs met. Without even knowing it.

Clara continued this pattern until she began to see what she was doing, and started to reflect on the types of partners she was attracting and why. She made a declaration that she no longer needed to date men who needed her. She didn't want to mommy a man—she wanted to worship a King.

She stopped going after the starving artist archetype, and started to date men who truly didn't need her. Men who indeed had money, decent jobs and lush social lives. That, in itself, was uncomfortable. She would think to herself, "What are they doing with me if they don't *need* me?" This was the real worthiness wound that needed to be felt.

So she felt it—and felt it fully. She went through a year of looking at her worthiness wounds, which required also looking at her relationship with her mother. Clara began to mother herself in the way she wished that she was mothered. She held herself through her tears, began to redesign her home in a way that felt nurturing and cozy, and learned how to cook *just for herself.*

Clara didn't need to take care of a man. She needed to take care of herself. And through the process of taking care of her own body, heart and soul, she began to deepen her confidence and self-love. She no longer had the time or energy to date men who dragged her down and needed her. She had a life to live!

She is now in a happy, healthy, stable relationship with a man who makes multiple-six-figures and has a house he *put her in*, rather than wanting her to put him in something. Through embodying the Queen, she manifested her King.

NEEDS AS A COMPASS

To reaffirm, having needs is okay. You just want to have sovereignty over whatever needs you have. For Clara, she didn't stop having needs altogether…her needs simply shifted from a low vibrational state (needing to feel needed) to a high one (needing to feel *wanted*). Feel the difference?

And let's be super clear—you are not needy for having needs. These are two completely separate things.

The term neediness refers to the energy someone gives when they are grasping *outwardly* to fill, fix or avoid an inward experience, rather than relaxing and opening through the longing. Neediness is what happens when one cannot sit with the intensity of their own feelings and uses others to make it go away.

Neediness can be a useful indicator of how deeply your own needs are not being met, and therefore, it's counter-productive to shame your own neediness. It's a compass.

My needs in relationship shifted from needing to be *controlled* into needing to be *loved* for my many forms of self-expression. Because expressiveness was such a challenge growing up that it's become my life's work (aka this book). I'm not insinuating that my partner can't have hurt feelings if I do or say something that hurts him because I expect him to love everything I do, but rather, that he can be with the hurt and bring it to me while also being open to my expression being messy. In summary, I need to be in a relationship that doesn't demand perfection and instead, appreciates individuality.

By choosing a partner who lifts up my unique form of expression, I am literally rewiring the original wound in my family. My nervous system is getting used to having my self-expression to be *loved* rather than despised. Relationships can be used as the deepest healing tool for this reason, but it requires you to first look at the needs yourself.

As a woman, I needed to become my own number one cheerleader in regards to self-expression so that I could call in a person who would also serve as a cheerleader for self-expression. Before looking for a partner to fill the role, I needed to fill it.

I filled this role by expressing myself out of the wazoo: amplifying my reactions with friends, vocalizing my needs, creating artistic videos, making comedic skits, writing poetry, gifting whomever I was dating with my heart in the ways that felt aligned to me, saying no when I meant it, asking for what I wanted when I realized it, ending half-hearted connections the minute I saw they judged me in unhealthy ways, and dressing in ways that made me feel like the goddess *I wanted to be.*

Where do you still need to love yourself? Where do you still need to honor your experience or emotions? Where do you still need to nurture and re-parent yourself?

The answers to these questions will point directly to the needs you can begin to embody yourself so that you can move forward, onto bigger and better things. The more you ignore a need, the more you'll stay wrapped around its little finger, spiraling deeper and deeper into neediness or self-blame. On the flip side, the minute you create something with it, you begin to reverse the power. You are now on the throne, dear Queen!

Here are a few examples of experiences and the needs available behind them.

- **Experience:** feeling gut-wrenching longing for the boyfriend of your dreams. Need: an outlet to express and be witnessed in the open-hearted love you are ready to give.

- **Experience:** feeling shame for parts of yourself you don't like. Need: a ritual that ceremonially gives these parts of yourself an opportunity to be held so that they can move and pass through.

- **Experience:** feeling insecure or worried about people you love eventually leaving you. Need: using tools such as dancing, writing and acting to give the insecure one in you a voice.

- **Experience:** feeling frustrated that someone you love keeps belittling you. Need: learning healthy ways to reveal how their unconscious tactics make you feel, for as long as you choose to be in relationship with them.

You do not need to be in a relationship to be an artist of love, as the most important element is to start with making art as a woman *for* Woman. The artistry of love is about this alchemy. Turning shit into serenity! Wounds into wonder! Resentment into RaInBoWs! Art through millenia, back to cave drawings and beyond, has always been rooted in storytelling. And while this chapter isn't about *making* art per say, I believe embodying needs is a form of art. It requires feeling deep emotions, creating nurturing environments, detoxing from toxic relationships and filling your life with goodness that is unique to you. All of that is artistic.

JUST AN ARCHETYPE
AND HER ART

While the four archetypes will feel absolutely delicious to a partner, they're more importantly going to feel delicious to YOU. You deserve the experience of feeling and reclaiming all these powerful bits and pieces of your heart. You deserve this level of intimacy and artistry, given to you by you.

The glorious thing about getting needs met by yourself is that it doesn't require you to receive anything outside of you, but rather *create* something from within. Talk about a dream scenario for the woman who is ready to take back her power! Let's take a look at each archetype and how they create art to meet their own individual needs.

LOYAL ORACLE

Out of all four archetypes, the Loyal Oracle is the most giving. Not only is she skilled with physical gifts, but she is divinely resourced in the emotional depth department.

The highest manifestation of a Loyal Oracle's gift is that she can always be counted on to unveil the deepest truth, and call in the highest level of integrity from those around her. To be in a relationship with someone who is embodying the Loyal Oracle is to be in relationship with growth itself. She will always call you into deeper realms of integrity.

That said, there is a shadow side to the gifts of the Loyal Oracle too. When her gift of loyalty stands alone *without* her gift of individual wisdom, she will give and give and give—so much that she can *merge* with others rather than setting healthy boundaries. *She doesn't know where her body stop and another starts—it's all swirling together.* *This* often looks like listening to the words of others over her own intuition. When somebody says "Jump!" she asks, "How high?" rather than, "Hmm, do I even want to jump? Does jumping feel like the most aligned decision for me? Do I trust the container to hold me in my jumpingness? Is their command to jump coming from a conscious place that feels respectful for me?"

Therefore, the deepest need of the Loyal Oracle is to be loyal to herself first and foremost.

Because her strongest gift is her foresight, it's important for the Loyal Oracle to tend to the part of her that is, well, the Oracle. The one who can see, feel and live beyond the veil. The one who knows there's more than what meets the eye.

I have a client named Teddi who, for much of her life, did not trust her intuition or wisdom. She was loyal, yes, but to all the wrong people.

She found herself flocking to untrustable, emotionally unavailable men who would consistently retrigger her deepest core wound in love—emotional unavailability. She would find men who felt a lot like her absent and unavailable father, hoping they would love her in the way he never could.

But because she wasn't actively practicing boundary setting and fine-tuning her radically awesome (but deeply buried) gift of intuition, she kept finding herself staying in these negative dynamics way past their expiration dates and feeling unmet in love. Time and time again, Teddi would find herself begging these unavailable men to take the relationship more seriously and finally commit. But they rarely did, and not for long.

THE LOYAL ORACLE MAKING ART

The Loyal Oracle's creative strategy is gift-giving, and the flavor she invokes is her raw heart.

When it came time for Teddi to walk the path of an artist of love and heal the wound she had around being worthy of commitment, she had to start with creating art by herself and only for herself.

Invoking the Loyal Oracle archetype, she decided to access her raw heart and give herself a few healing gifts to remind herself that *her* needs are priority. Here are a few ways she created gifts for herself:

* Creating a care package for herself filled with all of the things she would need next time she forgot the truth of who she is (which is a Mother Fucking Queenly Goddess of Divinity and Love). Her package included a vintage mirror (for seeing herself clearly), a quartz crystal ball to meditate into, a velvet blanket to wrap herself up in and a card to her future self she could read over and over.

* Making a special playlist, hand-crafted with all the music that lifts her spirits and gets her hips moving. As important as it is for the Loyal Oracle to feel the depths of her feelings, she also needs to remember to dance, play and express the *light* side of life.

* Going to a special pottery class where she made a pair of unique mugs that she and her future King would one day sip coffee out of together on their patio. Seeing these two mugs in her cupboard every day reminded her of the dream she was actively manifesting through her longing.

- Creating a vision board filled with images of different couples that represented the kind of love she wanted to call in. This creative project instantly gifted her with a state of yummy possibility, deep knowing and a strong vision of the love *she* wanted.

Each one of these pieces of art were about her meeting herself in the most tender of her experiences. After fully exploring the gifts of her own inner Loyal Oracle, Teddi was able to gain clarity on all the ways she was ignoring her intuition and listening to others before herself. She finally looked at her own lack of commitment to her *own* desires, and began to get super-duper clear on the kind of man — and partnership — she wanted.

Teddi ended the half-hearted, loose-end relationships that were dragging on as she bravely stepped into the unknown. She was ready to fully commit to what she wanted, which was an act of fully committing to herself. She took care of her own heart in the way her absent father didn't, thereby healing her nervous system wounds around abandonment and unworthiness. She *became* her greatest supporter through the process of looking at how she hadn't been.

After deep reflection, art creation, and distraction clearing, she was able to create space for a man with true blue, divine emotional availability…a firefighter named Lex. This man stole her heart at a neighborhood gathering, showed the fuck up for her feminine emotions and longings from day one, and was on board to build a serious commitment to and with her. They are currently engaged to be married with a baby on the way.

PLAYFUL PRIESTESS

The Playful Priestess can be considered the enlightened drama queen. She thrives on any kind of moment that is *amplified* — she lives for the theatrics of life.

The highest manifestation of the Playful Priestess is when she is actively stoking her own playful fire. Those who are in a relationship with her know that there is deep medicine in the art of letting down your hair, kicking off your shoes and running into an ocean for moonlight skinny dipping. In a world full of spreadsheets, tactics, defense mechanisms, force and fragility, the Playful Priestess is an angel of levity. She has a true gift for helping others loosen their white-knuckle grasp on life, which in turn, creates a deeper pathway for love to flow.

The shadow side of the Playful Priestess is when she caves into the way the rest of the world thinks she should be living her life, rather than following the beat to her own unique drum. Many Playful Priestesses grew up with the "silly girl!" wound, meaning they were shamed by one or both of their caretakers for having imaginary friends, unusual interests, or levels of energy on either end of the spectrum (high or low).

If a Playful Priestess hasn't worked on her childhood wounding around being told she's so "different" and how *bad* that is, then she's going to unconsciously grow up and try to find the most boring, routine, standard career out there. She will try to fit herself into, yet again, another box that was not made for her extra bright, big, bodacious, full, sparkly life.

There is *no* box fit for a Priestess.

The Playful Priestess must remember that it is her responsibility to *create* the energy she desires to see in the world—and to do so, she must walk the path of She Who is Different. She was not made to fit in—and if she continues to live in a world that "demands" it of her, she will ultimately suffer, grow bitter and disappear into the threads of our hyper driven society. Therefore, the deepest need of the Playful Priestess is to accept her own individuality.

But she absolutely *must* weed out the relationships that demand her to be different, less than or watered down. She is to become a shield maiden of her own energy, fighting out the stories, beliefs and nonsensical demands that were never hers to carry.

Here's an example: my client Jenny has a successful online business teaching women about marketing and making moolah. But for a long time the fear of losing followers, money or respect kept her from bringing the goofy, fun, humorous woman she is IRL to that business.

The identity split was painful. She *hated* having to put on her "Marketing Jenny" face and then turn it off to become her "Jenny-Jenny" self. She was walking on eggshells with her own damn self, a problem that is all too common for a Playful Priestess archetype.

THE PLAYFUL PRIESTESS MAKING ART

The Playful Priestess's creative strategy is drama and the flavor she invokes is playfulness.

Since the Playful Priestess was clearly holding some deep medicine for Jenny, I gave her a few assignments to invoke the essence of her inner priestess. Here are some ways Jenny created art with herself through her knack for drama and play:

* Whenever she received nasty comments from strangers on the internet, she made art out of it instead of internalizing and collapsing in on herself like she was taught to do as a child. Jenny began to make little videos doing "impressions" of what these people were like in real life by dramatizing, amplifying and animating every obnoxious thing about this internet troll, and either posted it bravely or put it inside of a special little folder on her computer to watch whenever she needed to remember *not* to hold back. "Debra from Doodledorf Road" was not worth collapsing in on herself for.

* She bought a special pair of hot pink sequin leg warmers to wear whenever she was in a particularly bad mood. Even if life was getting to her, she was going to shine like a million rosy suns.

- She created a special dance playlist specifically for mornings, which always set her up for a particularly joyful day. She committed to a 30-day practice where she would dance to at least three songs (usually with her dog on her hip) before opening her work emails.

- She created a monthly ritual where she would have a high-end bottle of rosé champagne delivered to her home to celebrate completing the month — any month. This was not something she would need to earn, she spent this extra money on herself no matter what, and who she was going to share it with was always part of the fun.

Each one of these examples reflected a way that Jenny could remind herself of who she really is. She's not a carbon copy of society — she is a divinely inspired priestess of play.

These assignments led her to blending more and more of "Marketing Jenny" with "Jenny-Jenny" until they became the same person. Unsurprisingly, she had an influx of new clients over the course of our work together — people who consistently wanted to work with Jenny because they related to her playfulness. Over the course of a year, she had to double her rates because she was receiving so many inquiries and could only work with so many people at once.

EROTIC ENCHANTRESS

The Erotic Enchantress is designed to follow the pulse of her pleasure. Since birth, she has been led by her innate erotic compass. She does not obsessively seek, force or hustle for things she logically wants, but rather, she is magnetized to whatever is meant for her through her erotic aliveness.

For the Erotic Enchantress, sex is a way of life — not just a thing she "does." She sees all of life through the lens of sacred union, eros, passion, fire, heat and luxury. The highest manifestation for an Erotic Enchantress is when she realizes she already *is* sex. There is no need to grasp or fill her seemingly insatiable hunger because she lives in the space of delicious eroticism already. Life is filling her constantly and because of this, she does not *need* to be filled by anyone. She already is filled by herself—and she loves it.

The shadow side of the Erotic Enchantress is when she does *not* cultivate her ability to feel life penetrating her, nor does she take the time to tend to her own realm of pleasure. When an Erotic Enchantress shuts off her five senses, shames her turn-on, lives from her mind instead of her pussy, and/or reaches outward to fix an inward longing, she will feel disempowered, frustrated and needy.

For example, if a girl was raised to shut down her sexuality at a young age, it's very likely she reversed that incredibly potent life force and internalized it as something that was shameful about her. This is exactly what leads to the grasping "neediness" as an adult—it's simply an unconscious tendency to quickly *do* something that will mute the sensation of yearning or pleasure.

And this internalized shame can manifest itself on either end of the spectrum—to avoid pleasure or become addicted to it. If you were shamed for your sex as a girl, you could have a food, sex or shopping addiction just as much as you could be depressed, avoidant or anxious.

If an Erotic Enchantress wants to create her own path to liberation, healing and abundance, it *has* to include deconstructing the internalized shame that was never hers to carry.

Sexuality is her birthright. Pleasure is her life force. Her sex is about her—for her. Yes, she will share it with lovers or perhaps one specific beloved, but her sexuality is not owned by anyone else...even in marriage. If someone enters her life who tries to dictate how or when she feels pleasure, it is a good opportunity for her to rise up into her power and stand up to (or step away from) that kind of patriarchal energy. The deepest need of the Erotic Enchantress is to embrace her own sexual nature as *pure*.

My student Lena was born as an incredibly beautiful baby—bright blue eyes, golden curls and rosy cheeks. From a young age, her father's friends would try to "connect" with her by saying things like, "Well hi there missy. You sure are beautiful, do you have a boyfriend?" followed by chuckles and a pat on the back.

This kind of interaction was highly uncomfortable for her at such a young age, but it was so normal and socially acceptable (and still is in some parts of the world) that nobody put a stop to it. It was the way things were.

Lena grew up in Alabama: a place that simultaneously exploited and shamed her beauty. She grew up hearing her parents talk about certain female celebrities being "such sluts" and how they were always "asking for it." Her parents made her do the bend-over and sit-down test when they went shopping to ensure there was never any cleavage in her tops or crackage revealed out of her pants.

Being monitored and objectified by her parents was not only invasive but also humiliating. There was very little room for her to come into her *own* body.

As an adult, Lena gained weight as a method of self-protection. She was exhausted with having to monitor her body or be responsible for the urges of men, so she shut down her own sexuality in efforts to protect herself.

THE EROTIC ENCHANTRESS MAKING ART

The Erotic Enchantress's creative strategy is dance and the flavor she invokes is eroticism.

Lena's journey to healing, self-love and sensuality was a long one that included multiple modalities, such as talk therapy and meditation, but creativity was the way she *alchemized* her pain and truly moved it forward.

Here are some ways Lena created art with herself through her gift of eroticism, sensuality and dance:

- Transforming her bedroom from a regular ol' place she sleeps into a sexual *palace*. Silk sheets, feathers, ropes, toys, lace and color-changing light bulbs filled every inch of her bedroom — all for herself.

- Creating a video log of her journey into body acceptance through dance. She invested in a beautiful ornate mirror that took up her entire wall and committed to a daily practice of erotic, seductive dance. Every day, she chose an outfit that her inner enchantress wanted to wear and danced slowly, sexually and deliciously for herself.

- Writing a short "fiction" story about a peasant woman who internalized and collapsed from her own power living in a village of sex-fearing, witch-burning idiots — and how she reclaimed it through fucking her way through an entire village and eating her victims afterwards. Total dream revenge.

- Creating sex magic rituals and completely *committing* to the theater of it. Knowing that she was an Erotic Enchantress she wanted to invest time, energy and love into using her gift of eroticism to create the life she was hungry for, so she invested in teachers who could show her this lineage. After learning many sexual rites of passages and rituals, she not only *did* them (yay for devotion!) but she committed to the entire process from the outfits and adornments she wore, the setting of the room, the music, the candles and every other piece of the scene.

Lena discovered that the comments and remarks of others, while patriarchal and annoying, were no reason she should neglect her own right to embody her bliss. That was, in every way, the patriarchy *winning*. And she was not going to let that happen.

Through connecting with her sexuality in the safe spaces she created for herself, she was able to bring more sensitivity back into her body. And because she was able to create intimacy with herself and actually *receive* that intimacy instead of internalize or deflect it, she began to feel satiated.

Lena lost twenty pounds that year (without counting a single calorie) since food was no longer her main source of intimacy, and started to shop for clothing that reflected the Erotic Enchantress within her. She came full circle by allowing her appearance to be just as vibrant and alive as the inside state she had cultivated. She began to love and appreciate the attention she received from others because it was something deeper this time — she was being recognized for her radiance, not just beauty.

At last, she loved being seen in the world.

SACRED DEVOTEE

Nobody is as attuned, refined and meticulous as the Sacred Devotee. In everything she does, there is a golden thread of sacredness: the way she eats, the way she makes love, the way she dresses, the way she runs errands, the way she rises each morning and goes to bed each night. It's all a ritual. It's all in devotion to *remembering* the truth of who she is: love.

In her highest manifestation, she does everything in pure devotion to love above all — which includes how she tends to herself. She knows that her own success and joy is *a part* of the success of love, and therefore, she is devoted not only to her practices, partner, beliefs, and friends, but also to her own needs and desires. She knows that her personal relationship with God, Goddess, the Divine, is priority… and it's only whenever she lets her practices slide that she begins to lose her footing.

If a Sacred Devotee relies on having a partner in order to feel her own devotion, she will feel disempowered, develop co-dependent behaviors, and jump from relationship to relationship just to make sure she can experience her devotional heart.

When this happens, another tricky aspect of the Sacred Devotee's shadow side can emerge. She begins to mistake her devotion for *perfection*. In order to find Mr. Right, she may lose contact with the purity of her devotional heart, and unconsciously manipulate it so that it looks a certain way in order to impress. Instead of moving from the longing of her heart, she moves from the calculations of her brain. There is nothing more soul-draining than this! Therefore, the deepest need of the Sacred Devotee is to remain in connection with god/dess no matter what shifts in her external circumstances.

The Sacred Devotee must learn that her discipline, her practices, her rituals and her ceremonies come from her heart and her heart alone.

My student Violet was, for as long as she could remember, drawn to ancient and holy rituals. She would sign up for course after course about priestess arts and tantric studies—she loved to learn about all the ways mystics have served God and Goddess throughout the ages.

That said, it was only when Violet was in partnership that she really embodied this way of living. Only then would she take the time to create sacred spaces, ask for morning eye contact, prepare evening chanting for the two of them, and even ceremonially wash and massage his feet after a long day at work. When they made love, she would sing into his genitals and let every move of her hips be in devotion to the Beloved.

Problem was, the men she would date weren't all about this lifestyle. They couldn't really *meet* her in the rituals and appreciate the level of devotion she would bring. Because of this lack of compatibility, the partnerships would inevitably come to a close. When this happened, Violet would become perfectionistic, fear-driven, lazy and self-doubting. She would stop creating daily ceremonies and instead get lost in hours of reality television. Instead of creating sacred spaces for herself, she would get obsessed with cleaning and organizing her apartment. Her longing was *so* intense that without an outlet or creative pathway for it, it became internalized and collapsed in on her.

Something I've seen a lot of women do is rely on a man in order to "feel their feminine." Therefore, when they are not in a relationship, they go into hyper-masculine states or, like Violet, hyper-avoidant states. They choose making sales pages over enjoying self-seduction, or spreadsheets over sheepskins. They get into cleaning or organization obsessions rather than sacred space creations.

While this is okay for a period of time, if you get lost here for weeks or months, then *of course* you will jump into any relationship in order to feel your feminine essence again. A huge piece for the Sacred devotee to learn is how to be in devotion to her feminine *especially* while single — this is going to be the make-or-break in regards to whether you jump into another partnership with someone who can't match your exquisite essence with his own.

THE SACRED DEVOTEE MAKING ART

The Sacred Devotee's creative strategy is ceremony and the flavor she invokes is devotion.

As is the case for all four archetypes, you can only embody your gifts in *love* to the extent that you can in your *aloneness*. If you drop your practices the minute you're single, you will not have them fully developed in partnership. And trust me, things get a lot more complicated when there's two instead of one!

As a budding artist of love, you must make it your sacred priority to embody the truth of who you are, regardless of who is around. This is the foundation that everything you receive in partnership will be built upon.

Here are some ways Violet created art with *herself* through her flavor of devotion to get back in touch with who she really is:

* Creating a magical self-marriage ceremony. Laying out multiple luscious sheepskin rugs in a candlelit room, she read aloud her handwritten vows and anointed herself with oils and rose petals.

* Trading out her dining room table in her small one-bedroom apartment for a small ceremony table she could sit at for tea, pulling tarot cards and chanting with her harmonium. As much as having a table was nice for guests, what *she* wanted was a sacred space to enjoy her daily ceremonies, and that was much more important to her than a dining room table. What the Sacred Devotee wants, the Sacred Devotee gets!

* Going to a local jewelry-making workshop and creating an anklet bracelet purely in devotion to the part of her that is ancient and mystical. Every time she put it on, she instantly felt like Mary Magdalene preparing to wash the feet of Jesus with her hair and perfume!

* Making altars around her entire home to fill every inch with deities, gods and goddesses she adores. This small but simple act was in itself an act of devotion. Not only is she now constantly reminded of those she loves, but by seeing these images her heart is in a constant state of worship!

By slowing down and unearthing new levels of her intentionality *for* herself and *with* herself, Violet activated her unwavering devotion muscle as an artist of love. She felt her devotion completely on her own, with the invocation of god/dess in her heart, and chose to be completely fulfilled as a single woman for a year. She wanted to learn that she didn't need to be in partnership just to feel her devotion. She wanted to be with someone who could finally appreciate her devotional gifts and be equally as devotional in return.

A lot of women associate long periods of being single with being lonely. But not for Violet—that year was epic. She traveled to India, got a life coaching certification, made a gorgeous website with beautiful photos, adopted a labradoodle, made peace with her estranged mother and went to a yoga retreat in Mexico. She directed her devotion to herself to be a better woman, and succeeded.

For as long as you associate being single with being bored or lonely, you will jump from relationship to relationship without being fully in devotion to your path. In the periods of singlehood, use your time to get in alignment with the woman you want to be *for you*. Create ceremony and rituals! Embark on pilgrimages and journeys! Your dream beloved will meet you from *that energetic state* over being relationship-addicted and lonely.

PRACTICE: TURNING "HER" ON

This is a practice that will support you in unifying yourself with the archetype you want to embody. By toggling between "you" and the archetype, you will be able to feel and inhabit the archetype with greater agency. You'll know *how* to turn her on because you have practiced. Read through these instructions at least one time fully before doing the practice so that you can do it without reading.

Find a private space in your home, preferably a bedroom, and turn on some music that reflects the archetype (pop or tribal beats for the playful priestess, sexy music for the erotic enchantress, etc.). Start by sitting on a chair or the edge of your bed and close your eyes.

Feel one of these archetypes inside of your heart (pick the one that feels the most enlivening in this moment—you can always do the others later).

Notice the five senses, internally: What does she smell? What taste is in her mouth? What does she hear? What does she look like? How does her body feel?

Staying with her, open your eyes and notice the five senses, externally: What does she smell in your room? What does she want to eat? What kind of music does she want to hear? How would she like to be dressed today? How does she see her own body? What fabrics and textures would she like to touch? Experience the world through her body.

Now, close your eyes, drop the practice and go back to "you."

What do you smell? What taste is in your mouth? What do you hear? What do you look like? What do you feel like?

Notice what differences you feel. What changed? What shifted? Did your shoulders drop? Did the position of your head shift? Do you feel less or more excited? Without any judgment, go back through your senses and notice how things are different or similar.

Now, keeping your eyes closed, turn her back "on."

Feel her once more—go back into the five senses.

Now, amplify the experience by making sound. Purr, growl, sigh, whisper, sing, hum. Don't overthink it. Let her lead you in sound. After a couple minutes, start to amplify. Get a little louder, and let yourself experience pleasure in the vibration of your throat.

Practice turning *on* and *off* your archetype two more times, while keeping your eyes open this time. (If you have a mirror, go stand in front of it for this part.) Fluctuate between making sound and moving with pleasure as the archetype, to dropping the practice and being with yourself.

Watch what literally shifts in your body (you'll be surprised how much of a difference you will see in your body by shifting energetic states).

Close the practice after ten minutes of toggling between the two energetic states and end with a bow to yourself in the mirror. Bow to you—and bow to her *within* you.

If you feel comfortable, you can begin to practice turning "on" the archetypes at different places such as the grocery store, at a party or even at your work (letting it be very, very subtle if you are in a male-dominated environment).

Have fun with this one—you're getting to know different parts of yourself.

Don't hesitate to wine and dine the luxurious Oracle, Priestess, Enchantress and Devotee within!

FROM ARCHETYPES TO CHARACTERS

The four archetypes will give you a sound launch pad for your artistry, but what if you want to go beyond only four options and into the great, endless landscape of the imagination? Where you turn four options into four hundred? Nay, four *thousand*!?

The next step is to look at the media, and the characters we see in it, as archetypes as well. You can become an artist of love by invoking characters from movies and observing how they walk, talk, speak, dress, make love, display joy, embody excitement and more. Characters have so much to teach us! From the brilliance of Elizabeth Bennet to the hopelessly devoted heart of Sandy Olsson to the ferocity of Maleficent to the airy-fairy nature of Luna Lovegood… you have *all* of these energies within you, even if you don't currently feel them.

By learning monologues, scripts and scenes from characters, you can *invoke* them into your daily life to bring more of you online in both life so you can bring more online in love.

Remember, all humans desire range, both inside themselves and in their partnerships. Everyone wants to experience the entire universe inside themselves—and characters *aid* us in that magical, imaginative process. In the next chapter, we will take a look at one of my favorite practices for invoking characters as a feminine embodiment practice.

MONOLOGUES AS A
SPIRITUAL PRACTICE

Monologues are long, uninterrupted speeches. Anytime an actor takes their time to share a pivotal experience or an emotional revelation, they're probably giving a monologue. It's their big, bright, shiny moment!

The profound beauty of a monologue is that it offers an arc: the beginning, middle and end all feel, sound and look different. The character goes through a journey in and of itself when a monologue is spoken. There's an inherent *range*, even if the speech is only a few minutes in length.

Learning a monologue is a practice anybody can do, no matter where they are in their artistic journey. Even if you are a seasoned actor and have learned a thousand monologues, learning one as a spiritual practice can bring fresh energy, inspiration and creativity into this practice for you as a woman — not just as an actor.

Because a monologue already provides a masculine structure (the words), all you have to do is allow yourself to be affected by what you're saying as truthfully as you can (the feeling). Can you feel the truth of what you're saying and how it relates to your own life? Can you let what you're saying stir your heart strings? Can you allow yourself to feel joy bubble up? Jealousy? Longing? Rage? Regret?

By taking time to study something as simple as a monologue, you can create a deeper and wider range as a lover in your real life. You can use this acting modality as a practice in expanding your capacity to *feel*. Feeling is the feminine; she is energy in motion. Emotion. When you give a monologue you are embodying that emotion, and allowing it to sweep you away, if only momentarily.

THE MEDICINE OF JOAN OF ARC

When I began exploring acting for the first time in New York City, the first monologue assigned to me was Saint Joan (Joan of Arc).

I spent weeks laboriously memorizing the words on the page, without much attention to the feeling within the words. So when it came time to "perform" my monologue, the words were empty and my energy was stale.

My teacher, who was also a friend, took me through three rounds of embodying Saint Joan in different ways to support me in accessing the *feelings* underneath the words.

The version that stood out the most was when he told me to stick out my tongue and raise my hands into the air between every line, as if I was Kali.

Kali is a Hindu goddess known for being a master of death, destruction, time, change and liberation. She is the Great Mother, always obliterating obstacles getting in the way of love. Kali is a somewhat vicious looking blue skinned goddess with long black hair and her tongue sticking out. Every aspect of Kali is deeply symbolic, so while she may seem scary, she is profound medicine. She is the dark feminine, embodied. Brave, fierce and relentless (all in the name of love, of course).

My range as a woman was solid in the "love and light" department (maiden, devotional wife, sacred groupie, teacher's pet). But I was weaker in my development of the dark feminine department (justice-seeking warrior, femme fatale, dominatrix, bossy pants, big bad bitch).

And if I couldn't accept my own ferocity, how far could I really go with the warmth I wanted to use to change my corner of the world?

How tall could I really stand?

How embodied could my voice really get if I was too afraid of my own depths?

How strong of an imprint could I make in the rooms I enter if I have to tip-toe around with a constant stream of "please and thank you?"

How could I ever call my masculine partner deeper into his own integrity if I couldn't also stand up to him? Stand up *for* him?

By combining the *energy* of Kali and the *words* of Joan of Arc to work with, I was able to explore a repressed side of my psyche that I needed to liberate.

"Yes, they told me you were fools, and that I was not to listen to your fine words nor trust to your charity," I said, and stuck out my tongue to breathe fire.

"You promised me my life; but you lied. You think that life is nothing but not being stone dead!" I said, and raised my arms in the air as if I was preparing myself for battle. And on and on I went.

By the end of the monologue, I was feeling heat in my fingers, fire in my womb and power in my throat. My friend said, "Great, now go through it again and drop the physicality of Kali. Just feel it."

I went through the monologue, full of fire and passion, feeling my entire body turn into Joan of Arc...but as *Madelyn*. I could feel the one in me who *was* Saint Joan. Who would fight for my dignity in the face of men in court.

Who would go into battle for God. Who felt betrayal running through her bones. I felt *transformed*.

That very same energy I experienced rushing through my body was now *a part of me*. There was before-monologue-Madelyn and then there was after-monologue-Madelyn. And after-monologue-Madelyn was the only Madelyn available now.

My body had received a transmission — an *embodiment* — that was now coded within my DNA. I had a brand-new neural pathway forming between my nervous system and my innate ferocity, ready to be whipped out and utilized at a moment's notice.

Somebody manipulating me into thinking I'm less than the stellar queen I am? *I got this.*

Somebody bullying me on my Instagram? *Bitch I got boundaries!*

Somebody picking on somebody I love? *Hold my beer.*

Of course, more practice of this "sacred justice" was still necessary in order to fully embody and learn how to control this new energy... but that was a big first step, all those years ago.

And that's the power of a monologue.

If I simply regurgitated the words on the page, I wouldn't have been able to feel, nor reveal, the deeper range available in this monologue. Once I included my fingers, my tongue, my arms, my belly, my breath — the physicality of my body — *that* is when I could access the emotion. My chemistry, symmetry, biology and nervous system all collectively opened from that performance.

This level of heart-opening transformation via a monologue can happen for anyone who yearns to access deeper levels of their emotions, but needs a sturdy foundation set before them in order to get there.

Your process might look different than mine. It might take a while to find the first monologue. It might feel awkward to speak the words. You may become hyper aware of the weird angle of your legs as you speak, or become unsure of what to do with your hands. This is all normal.

The gift of the monologue is not the destination, it's the journey. So if you feel awkward can you speak the monologue *with* that awkwardness? If you feel insecure being someone you're not, can you speak the monologue *with* that insecurity? If you feel frustrated that this whole process is unfamiliar, can you *include* that frustration into every word? Whatever comes up for you on your journey to becoming a full-fledged, practicing, artist of love is a part of your feminine embodiment journey. Nothing is outside of it—even the sticky emotions.

After practicing your monologue(s) over a period of time (I would recommend at least two months), you may start to feel a difference in your "normal" self. You may have a little more pizazz, ferocity, depth, curiosity, innocence, bitch, bad girl, sensuality, sexuality, openness, rawness, or confidence, depending on the character you choose. The changes may be subtle, but don't drop the practice simply because you don't become a different human overnight. This work happens in layers—and it's primarily about integration. You are *integrating* a character within yourself that wasn't online previously. This takes time! Allow yourself to slow down and trust the process. In time, you will quite literally feel differences in how you exist in your own body.

CHOOSING A MONOLOGUE: LEVEL ONE

There are two ways you can choose a monologue.

The first way is to choose a monologue that feels like you. Find a character from a movie that you already deeply relate with. Maybe it's the love-struck gal from a romantic comedy, or the "fuck off!" rebel from an angsty teen film. Who do you see yourself in?

Choosing a monologue from a character you relate to is considered "level one" practice because you can already relate to the character's journey in at least some way. You'll be able to feel the character's truth without having to completely force or fake through it.

By choosing a monologue that you relate with, you don't have to dig *too* deep into the underbelly of your psyche, which can be helpful when you're just beginning to use monologues as a spiritual self-help practice. You can focus on the practicalities of the practice such as learning lines and feeling feelings. It's like doing a bunny slope before a black diamond—probably a good idea.

I run a yearly program called Creativity in Love where a small group of students dive into the deep end to explore and embody different archetypes and flavors of their feminine through acting, improvisation and shadow work. Towards the end of the program, I break up the larger group into smaller groups of three, and they work together to give each other (1) the texture that still needs to be integrated and (2) a character that embodies that texture.

After pinpointing the texture and character, each student prepares a monologue to perform near the end of the program as a way to celebrate the integration. They come to that class dressed as the character, in makeup and with all the props. It's a delight to see how everyone arrives to the call, committing to the theater of their texture!

One of my previous Creativity in Love students, Nikki, had a naturally powerful energy. She was endearingly sweet, yes, but something about her also felt inherently penetrating. Unfortunately, given that we live in a world where "power" has so many negative consequences for women (such as being called a bitch for being too direct), it was near impossible for her to find a safe space to practice embodying and liberating that inherent power. She was continuously watering down her power which led her to situations where she didn't speak her truth, didn't honor her inherent queenliness and didn't feel met in love.

On the day of performances, she said she would be invoking the texture of *commanding presence* as Daenerys Targaryen from *Game of Thrones*. She arrived at the call fully dressed in Daenerys's classic black uniform, sitting on a throne she created; the computer's camera was angled just a little bit below her throne, which gave the effect of us being smaller than her (little touches, like this, are important when creating a scene).

After her first performance (which was *amazing*), I invited a few students in the class to share feedback on what they believed would liberate She Who is Daenerys within Nikki even more for the second round. They all said the same thing: more *fire*.

Feel the fire in your belly. Feel the fire in your devotion. Feel the fire as the one and only, queenly, Mother of Dragons. Give us that *fire-breathing* passion!

They also suggested she narrow and dial in her focus through her eyes and posture. They requested everything in her body to be a little bit sharper, from an unwavering gaze to a set jaw.

Nikki slid back into her throne and performed the monologue a second time. This time, her gaze was sharper, her voice was deeper and the tension she created by pausing in between lines was more prominent. Using her body and energy alone, she *became* the fire. By merely invoking an natural element, like fire, she was able to double her power instantaneously.

Once completed, Nikki was smiling and radiantly open—the part of her that was fire-breathing passion was liberated in a way she didn't give herself permission to do before and the difference was *undeniable* to those playing witness!

After the practice, she went back into her life and invoked the power of Daenerys in the moments she felt the most ungrounded or unconfident. She shared with me that to this day, she will channel Daenerys when she feels unsure of using her voice, and she'll immediately feel her spine strengthen, and her words come out slower, with more clarity. The one in her who is the Mother of Dragons supports her in running her baking business, speaking her needs in her dating life and asking for what she wants out of life.

CHOOSING A MONOLOGUE: LEVEL TWO

The second choice is to choose a monologue that feels nothing like you. Pick a character that makes your stomach turn, blood boil and gag reflex *flex*. If there's any character you know of that disgusts, terrifies or repulses you in any way, they clearly hold an ingredient that you have shut off within yourself. There is medicine there.

Choosing a monologue from a character that repulses you will take you a bit further into the deep end of the pool. This is a good next step after you've familiarized yourself with the newness of learning a monologue and feel ready to go into some darker, stickier, crunchier territory.

This is what I consider to be *shadow work*. Shadow work, a term created by Carl Jung, refers to the exploration of your repressed aspects, behaviors and thoughts. While some shadow work is done in pure contemplation ("hmm I wonder why I'm such a bitch, let me think on that") the most effective kind is when you sovereignly act out your shadows in a container. By giving them a voice, a body and a moment under the spotlight, you get to liberate them from the shadows—and therefore, liberate yourself from their control.

And while a level two monologue will often bring some dread, it will *also* bring some joy. You have the stage to be all the things you were told you never could be in one single container. By having a "time and place" to step into these pieces, you receive permission to feel something fully because you know there will be a start *and* stop time. Knowing it's in a container makes all the difference to your psyche. *Anybody can go into something for three minutes!*

One of my students during the last cohort of Creativity in Love, Clarissa, was fairly reserved. Over the course of four months, she became more and more playful, open and embodied with the space. And yet, there was still a specific texture that wasn't getting touched by a ten-foot pole: her *nastiness*. The group wanted to feel the one in her who was bitchy, messy, raunchy and unabashedly bossy in the process. She was naturally sweet, pure and kind—but what's on the other side of that? And how much more embodied would all her other qualities be once she embraced the dark?

Though it wasn't a monologue (*naughty!*), Clarissa chose the song *Poor Unfortunate Souls* from Ursula in The Little Mermaid. This choice made her *gulp* just a little more than a level one monologue would, because not only was she playing with an *energy* that is nasty (which went against everything she stood for) but also because she was becoming a character that's big, bad and brutal. Ursula is a repulsive choice for someone who has a conscious desire to be seen as good, kind and friendly.

But what's on the other side of that repulsion? Say it with me—*LIBERATION!*

You can only embody your brilliant, juicy *lightness* to the extent you're familiar with your murky, underbelly *darkness*. To be liberated into the woman you truly want to be, it requires a sacrifice of your ego, courage to face the unknown and a willingness to let go. You have to know all sides of yourself in order to sovereignly choose who you want to be.

Alongside the *gulp* I also remember seeing a tidbit of excitement in making the choice to do Ursula. There was a small, hidden piece of her I hadn't seen before light-up ever so subtly. Her body released some energetic weight—as if her unconscious mind was saying, "Ah FINALLY I get permission to be bad!!!"

On monologue performance day, Clarissa arrived at the call with the perfect white Ursula wig, all the adornments, glitter blue eyeshadow, bright lipstick and the perfect *Little Mermaid* ocean virtual background. She brought the one in her who was catty, powerful, bitchy, and sacredly evil. As she sang her song, each student was lit up with so much joy and elation at seeing the Ursula in Clarissa. *Thereeeee she is!*

After she finished her song, we all delightfully applauded and created space for feedback before she went in for her second round. The group collectively asked for even more bitchiness, nastiness and self-righteousness—they invited her to make faces that demonstrated more disgust, and to use her hands as if she was wafting off the patheticness of all the poor unfortunate souls.

Clarissa went back into her song, with full permission to amp up the spite and pity, and a completely new part of her personality was—very apparently—unlocked. Her lips curled, eyes rolled, laughter deepened, and eyebrows narrowed. She accessed the one in her who was a true blue nasty bitch.

She has since told me that Ursula has done a great deal of things for her modern day life, including: no longer apologizing excessively or acting as if she is inconveniencing another when she has a basic request, no longer leaving her Zoom video on in work meetings that have nothing do with her, allowing herself to set boundaries with family members without falling into a "I'm bad" spiral, existing with more *audacity* and no longer playing a "background character" role in her own life and instead, stepping into the main character.

The point of this is not to *become* the shadow you're working with- in fact it's the opposite. People usually become the shadow from the sheer resistance of it. When you try so hard *not* to step on anyone's toes, be a bitch, or be whatever flavor you're avoiding, you struggle to ask for what you need out of fear of rejection. When you don't ask for what you need (but still need it), you use passive ways to get it—beauty, emotions, codependency, guilt-tripping, silent treatment, "losing trust," demanding people to read your mind, unconscious gaslighting, etc. You may think these tactics are better, but they're not — and for as long as you hide away from your bold confidence, you may continue to use these tactics that are watering down your power and manipulating people in the process.

Plus, imagine bringing these shadow sides into the bedroom! How fun and unexpected would it be for a beloved to experience his beautiful woman's unexpected nasty bitch come out paired with her good heart? It's hard to be with an unconscious bitch who is legitimately mean, but it's surprisingly delightful to be with a good woman who is playing *with* the energy of bitchiness. It adds a new flavor of excitement, and keeps the partner on his toes. It leads to a greater range available to play with in the bedroom, which makes everything spicier.

But… you have to get to *know* this part of yourself first.

By practicing with a monologue to feel and embody these pieces of yourself, you begin to create a relationship with them. The relationship you build with the thousands of different aspects of yourself is what will lead to sovereignty in *who* you want to be, *how* you want to be her and *when* you want to invoke her.

THE "HOWS" OF A MONOLOGUE

Here are some steps for you to take so you can get started on choosing and performing your perfect monologue.

1. Choose your character and monologue. The internet has thousands of these. If you merely search *funny female monologues, romantic female monologues* or *dramatic female monologues* you will find an entire archive of them. Alternatively, you can watch a movie that you love and type out the character's monologue, as they speak it, if you cannot find it online. I have done this on more than one occasion when I couldn't find something I really wanted to learn. It's a beautiful way to embody your devotion to the practice.

2. Memorize the lines. Before worrying about the *feeling* behind the words, just learn the words. In polarity, this would be the masculine structure—and having the masculine structure down is exactly what is going to allow the feminine emotion behind it to flow. I like to memorize my lines in two ways: firstly, I will record my monologue in my own voice (without *any* kind of emotion behind it—just the bare bone, plain words) and listen to it as I'm getting ready for the day, in my car and on my walks. The more I listen to it, the faster I memorize it. Another great way to memorize a monologue is to rehearse one line at a time. Read it on the paper, close your eyes and then read it out loud. Only once you can say the full line can you move on to the next line. You can have the entire monologue memorized in less than an hour doing it this way.

3. Pinpoint what the character *wants*. Lines are hardest to remember when you have no connection to the meaning behind the words, so know *why* you are saying what you're saying. For example, Joan of Arc wanted freedom and justice. Daenerys wanted the Iron Throne. Ursula wanted power and revenge. Create your own individual connection to the deepest desire of your character—do they want love? To be accepted? To get their money back? To feel safe? To get sex or validation? Identify it.

4. Perform the monologue, even if just in your bedroom, with different flavors and textures. Try it angry, devastated, in heat, frustrated, like you need to pee or just had a great orgasm, while laughing-crying, or like you just lost your job and nobody knows. Take whatever it is the character *wants* and pair it with different circumstances to see how it will come out.

5. You can allow the *pitch* to which you would say the monologue bleed into these moments of your life, too. Deepen (or raise) your voice, articulate your speech and speak from that place of your character.

It can be light, airy, fluffy, strong, verbose, vibrant, giggly, powerful or sing-songy. The pitch of your voice can change *a lot* about the energy you bring into your life. You can shapeshift as a feminine being purely by playing with the tone of your voice: try speaking breathy like Marilyn Monroe and you will *feel* sexier. Try speaking meticulously like any Angelina Jolie character and you will *feel* more powerful. Your tone is one of your greatest tools.

6. Use your body. Acting is not just about speaking, it's about *doing*. Show us how the monologue moves through your body—throw up your hands, spread your legs, slide your glasses up your nose, slam your hand on a table, lick the air, pick a wedgie, bite your lip. And then go again, making a completely new choice.

7. Create an arc. Discover how the beginning, middle and end of your monologue are all different for you, emotionally. Use pauses, vocal pitch, energy and physicality to create an arc in your monologue—there's nothing worse than when an actor (meaning *you* now) uses the same exact tone, in the same exact pitch, with the same exact energy the whole monologue through. Variety in a monologue, just like in the feminine, is key.

8. Perform it! Perform the monologue in front of friends, your women's group or just in front of your video camera. You can always record the monologue and send it to a few people you would love to have witness you in this energy. Having witnesses (an audience) is important when it comes to really instilling this energy within your nervous system. Being *witnessed*, *validated* and *acknowledged* are all a part of the artist of love's path to deeper healing and creativity.

9. Ask for feedback from your witnesses on what you could do to go deeper. Ask for a few *specific suggestions*—things you can physically do with your body. For example, doing something with your hands

that you didn't do in the first round. Squealing mid-monologue. Jumping up and down like a brat. Tightening or loosening your jaw. Moaning in ecstasy. One round of feedback to go deeper will do a lot for deepening the experience and expression.

INTEGRATION

As I mentioned earlier, learning a monologue is not going to feel the most natural if you've never done it before. Don't get too caught up in the whole, "But this isn't me! This doesn't feel authentic" bullshit. This is you. The entire concept of "this isn't me!" is society-made. *You* are limitless. *You* are everything.

In fact, a monologue practice will lead to feeling like that "inauthentic thing" is finally authentic. For example, if you want to be a spiritual coach, but you have imposter syndrome (aka you feel like an imposter every time you say you're a spiritual coach) it doesn't mean you're actually an imposter. It simply means you *feel* like an imposter. And feelings, as we all know, shift.

Just because you feel like you're pretending to be something for a period of time, doesn't mean you're being fake or an imposter. It means you are training. You are practicing. You are stretching your range as a human.

Identify the nutrient that you are gaining from the monologue. What's the thing you want more of that this monologue can help you find? More ferocity? More confidence? More tell-it-like-it-is-ness? More innocence? More tenderness? More vulnerability?

The next time in your life you want to *feel* that nutrient, you can use your monologue character to step into that emotion. You can quite literally channel that character in whatever is happening.

For example, if you have a monologue that offers you the nutrient of ferocity, like Maleficent, you can channel her the next time you need to set a fierce but loving boundary. If you have a monologue that offers you the nutrient of confidence, like Elle Woods giving her graduation speech, you can channel her the next time you give a public talk. If you have a monologue that offers you the nutrient of vulnerability, like Allie from *The Notebook*, you can channel her the next time you're having a hard time expressing your feelings to a lover.

Monologues are going to liberate the turned-off parts of you and bring them into the limelight. As a performer—and an up-and-coming show-stopper—you're going to have these crucial pieces of yourself integrated so they can *serve* you in creating the life you want, rather than *drain* you from the effort required to hide them.

Not only that, but monologues are going to make more of you available to love. When more of your innermost world comes online, more of you is brought to the table to be experienced. You're not just "Katie the therapist and mom"—you are Katie the Seductress, the Priestess, the Mermaid, the Goddess, the Brat…and more. Your eyes reveal different stories. Your heart emits different desires. You become a shapeshifter moment-to-moment, never not surprising your beloved. You are a woman who holds thousands of women in the body of one. It's impossible—*impossible*—to grow bored with your existence when you are literally every flavor, all the time. There's always a new avenue to explore, to deepen, to embody.

THE FEMININE
HEART OF AN ARTIST

The artistry of love is a spiritual practice for women to discover more of themselves—and relationship is the next evolution of that path. Romantic relationship is a way that we more deeply feel and see our own selves, because we are witnessing someone else feeling and seeing *us*. All of the work you do in this section is preparing you, and even calling in, what's to come—the artistry of love with a partner.

Since all energy is the feminine, every time you perform a monologue and practice invoking emotions, expressions and archetypes, you are increasing your feminine literacy and preparing for greater levels of polarity with that partner (whether you're with him now, or soon to be). The wider your feminine range is, the deeper you're able to polarize your partner into their masculine. This is where chemistry, sex and erotic tension is born.

EVERYTHING you do today is influencing what's to come!

But before looking at how feminine-masculine artistry is experienced in a relationship, let's look at what an integrated feminine and masculine looks like within you as a woman. The more understanding and autonomy, you have with this dynamic inside yourself, the more you will be able to translate it into your partnerships. After all, you can only take others as deep as you can take yourself.

Your inner feminine is devoted to love above all, whereas your inner masculine is devoted to purpose above all. Here are some traits that represent the part of you who is purely feminine:

* You find great pleasure in looking at the ins and outs of your romantic relationships to make sure your love feels as juicy and alive as possible.

* You find yourself wanting most everything to last *forever* (the great book, the sad film, the delicious meal, the pitter-patter of the rain, a relationship).

* You question and analyze little things in your relationship and are very sensitive to the subtle shifts in energy or moods.

* You experience pleasure when you express your feelings (crying, laughing, yelling, grieving).

* You can feel into many things happening at once (you can ponder your friend's latest problem at the same time that you feel into your newest desires at the same time that you think about what you want for dinner).

* You keep an internal list of things, whether helpful or harmful (all the beautiful things you see on a walk, all the things you love about your partner, all the ways your partner has let you down in the past, your favorite desserts and most despised chores).

* You can cry and laugh at the same time—and you secretly or not-so-secretly love to be held during such amplified experiences.

* You feel best when you make decisions based on your internal compass and gut feelings.

- You want to be filled. When you're conscious about your desire to be filled, you lean towards the upper spectrum like energy, love, divinity, genitals, emotions, pleasure and God. When you're out of sorts a bit, you may lean towards less enlivening methods like food, gossip, and shopping.

- You're more attracted to those who embody depth, leadership and consciousness rather than radiance, pleasure and energy.

The feminine is the energy most concerned with accumulating love in any given moment (rather than the masculine's prerogative of purpose). In a *healthy* manifestation, this looks like being fully responsible for creating that love within — and then blasting it out. You are self-generated love. You transmit love wherever you go through how you walk, how you gaze, how you talk, how you dance, how you live and how you make love. Using the artist of love archetypes as an example, the healthy feminine would constantly be in relationship with her artistic flavor as a way to creatively express her desire moment-to-moment.

The *unhealthy* feminine is looking to be filled with love from the outside world. So rather than invoking her artistic flavor as a way to fill herself first and foremost, an archetype in the unhealthy feminine energy would rely on the outside world to satiate her. This chase leads her to trade the beautiful gift of invocation with the short-term pleasure of a quick fix.

In *Sex and the City* Miranda Hobbes (a woman who holds a strong Loyal Oracle energy) offers us a beautifully complex example of primarily feminine being who lives in a masculine world that acts like a straitjacket to her yearning heart.

She has a strong work ethic and takes pride in her self-sufficiency, as she should, and yet…there is a deeper longing that she has to be vulnerable, seen and loved as the open-hearted woman she is.

One of my favorite episodes is titled *What's Sex Got to do With It?* In it, Miranda goes on a sex strike because of her many disappointing dating escapades, but quickly turns to chocolate cake to soothe her cravings (i.e. desire to be filled). Eventually she gets so fed up with her chocolate cake addiction that she throws the cake into the trash and then suspiciously approaches the trash again to take a piece out and eat it.

Recognizing her desperate level of hunger, she turns to her vibrator and ends the sex strike. In any event, there's an obvious need to be filled and she bops around from one thing to the next to find the best way to soothe that need.

Have you ever felt yourself needing attention so badly that you reached out to that totally lackluster, unimpressive Tinder date seeing if he wanted to grab a drink, simply because you needed to fill the void? Or have you ever found yourself snacking on chocolate into the wee hours of the night because you were craving connection but had none in sight?

The unhealthy feminine isn't wide or conscious enough to remain grounded whenever she feels painful longing and/or emptiness arise so she reaches for whatever is closest in order to feel filled with love — food, sex, shopping, people who are blatantly no good for her and gossip are all possible feasts for the wounded feminine. The *filling* (sex, shopping, food, boyzzz) helps her feel momentary relief.

The way that you can transform this wounded energy into the healthy manifestation of the feminine is through artistry. When you know how to create art out of your pain, you stop going back to quick fixes just because you can't be with your emotions. And a big piece of creating this art is being able to *hold yourself* through the creative process — this is where your masculine comes in.

I'll use my own healthy and unhealthy feminine as an example. A couple years ago, I was dating a man who had some of the most beautiful looks I'd ever seen in my life. He was a red-head (*my* Achilles' Heel) with lots of freckles and a tall, muscular dancer's body. He was kind, funny and witty. That said, he was also a devoted Atheist with a very strong aversion to all things spiritual. He didn't like my interest in astrology, my various altars, my deity statues, my belief in feminine-masculine energetics and my request to eye-gaze before making love. Basically, all things that truly make me *me*, he didn't want around.

But (*throwing hands wildly into the air and running into a field of daisies*) — I DIDN'T CARE!!!! He was so beautiful! So tall! So funny! *This can work, can't it?!*

I believed it could, so I tried. Every time we met up, I would get a little smaller, a little quieter, a little less visible. I would work *really fucking hard* not to mess up our connection by being, well, myself. When I'd want to talk about a new goddess I was ecstatically learning about, I'd zip it. When I'd want to invite him to a spiritual gathering where we could sing and dance together, I'd go alone. When I wanted to tell him about said spiritual gathering, I held back.

As exhausting as it was to constantly check myself in this way, I was so high on the thrill of "having" him, that I convinced myself I didn't need to have these huge parts of myself in the relationship.

Yet…there comes a time when every woman has to choose that enough is enough. She will have to come to her own conclusion that self-betrayal in exchange for the short-term satisfaction of a warm body in her bed just won't cut it anymore. She needs more out of this one life. And she'll make a big change to see to it.

And after a long time, I realized that's what I had to do.

HUSBANDING
YOUR FEMININE

When you make the commitment to no longer dismiss, refuse or silence parts of yourself in order to feel accepted, you may be uncomfortable as you endure some newfound growing pains. All of a sudden, you'll no longer be able to date that hot guy just because he's interested in you. You'll wake up and realize you need more, deeper, bigger! And that you'd rather be single than try to force something that requires you to *lose* pieces of yourself in the process.

Or, if you're in a devoted partnership, you may start to recognize all the places you're not feeling met and you'll deepen your devotion by making art to give the relationship a chance to uplevel its game.

The illumination on what's not working for you, regardless, may bring about a period of awkward separation from you and those around you. Your life may start to feel a bit lonelier as you transition from Before Art You to After Art You. From Box You to Boxless You. Even if you stay with a beloved, the simple awareness you now have around something that maybe you didn't clearly see before, will lead to a stumbly, fumbly period of inner growth.

During this time of tender vulnerability, you can begin to create a connection with your own masculine essence so that "he" can hold you through this transition. This process is called *husbanding your own feminine*.

Learning how to hold and *husband* your own feminine heart will support you in soothing any tendencies to get addicted to the thrill of shallow external attention. It will bring you back down to earth. It will help you feel connected to your strong-as-an-ox roots, rather than get flighty as you hot-air-balloon yourself all the way up into the sky.

In the last section, I shared with you how I was trying to force myself into partnership with someone who couldn't see me for who I was. While I could have continued to make art out of my situation, I realized that one of my main needs in partnership was to be with someone spiritual. My partnership with him helped me realize how it was actually a *non-negotiable prerequisite* to be with someone who understood me on a spiritual level. So yes, while art would have been a great practice, I wanted to focus on making it with myself—not with him. I wanted to prepare myself for the future man I would eventually be with who could *really* love me the way I wanted. I wanted—and needed—to stay in the artistry of love with myself, and therefore needed space from anyone who couldn't actively meet me there.

I ended the relationship with RedHead Achilles' Heel Man and started to go through my agonizing period of attention withdrawal. I became graspy and ungrounded. Reaching outside of myself, I searched in the dark for anything that would give me the experience of being satiated: fleeting attention from other men, redecorating my entire home, indulging a bit too much in wine, phone calls with friends, throwing away my entire closet in exchange for a new one. Note that these things are not inherently bad, they were simply coming from an internal, primal urge to avoid feeling my own longing.

Eventually, I saw what I was doing and took a pause. I fell to my knees and humbly invoked the support of my inner Sacred Devotee with a prayer. *Help me feel my longing,* I asked. I wanted to reconnect with spirit *through* my longing, not outside of it.

The following morning, I filled my day with spiritual practice including chanting, creating beautiful altars and filling a new journal with little love notes of longing to the *future* beloved I was calling in. I sat with my longing, rather than trying to avoid her.

And then, my Sacred Devotee showed me a ceremony she wanted me to do as a way to husband my own feminine in sacred marriage. I'm going to teach it to you now.

PART ONE: MEETING YOUR SACRED MASCULINE

As I've said, you have your own masculine even as a woman. But who is he? What does he look like? What does he smell like? Is he big like a hunky lumberjack or lean like a ninja? Does he have curly, flowing locks or has he gone full Charles Xavier? Does he feel penetrating like the sun or Zen like a peaceful garden?

The following exercise will help you to identify who this mystery man is so you can begin to create a devotional relationship with him as more than just an idea, but as a living, breathing partner.

- In your journal, write down the names of ten *men* you trust. These people can be characters, actors, artists, deities, historical figures, gods, archetypes or real-life friends. If they're a character, or someone you've never met before, that's perfectly fine—you don't have to actually trust them, but you at least trust the idea of them. The only rule is you cannot put down the name of an ex, someone you're currently dating or your actual partner. Here are some examples of men on my list: Yeshua, Krishna, Dionysos, Gandalf, Shiva, Liam Neeson, and a friend named David.

- From your list of ten, circle the top three who you feel the deepest intimacy (or perceived intimacy), connection and devotion with.

For me, that ended up being Yeshua, Shiva and Dionysos. Choose whomever from your list you feel an inherent spark with.

* Look at the qualities of your three men. What do they represent to you? Safety? Security? Wisdom? Love? Feel their essence around you and notice what happens to your own body. Do you feel relaxed and open? Trusting? Held? In love? Delighted? intrigued?

* For the next three days, practice "waking up" next to each one of them. What does your morning look like together? How does he treat you, and tend to your heart? How does he touch your body? Does he feed you grapes in bed? Does he penetrate your heart with his gaze? Does he *really see* you?

* After your three days spent with each masculine archetype, choose the one who brought your heart to life the most. Which one did you feel held, seen, loved, and open with? Which man *met you* in the ways you've always wanted to be met? He is your sacred masculine.

You can always change your sacred masculine as you change and grow as a woman. He may start out as an actor you know, but immediately change appearance once you identify the *feeling* you get with the actor. We can use actors, characters and deities as a diving board, and trust that if our sacred beloved shapeshifts in a new way, it's for the best. Trust the shift—you don't *have* to stick with the appearance of the character.

Remember that this sacred masculine archetype is here to remind you of the kind of love you are deserving of when you begin to feel graspy, confused and hopeless in the real world. He is your masculine, here to eternally wine, dine and love you like there is no tomorrow. He is your rock, your safe harbor. Your etheric hubby.

PART TWO: THE SACRED MARRIAGE

The reason why most relationships suffer is because both people in the partnership put loads of expectations on the other. They expect them to be *everything*—a best friend, a lover, a parent, a sibling, a financial adviser, a babysitter, a therapist, a devotee. It's a lot.

But what if you already had someone in your life that was all these things for you? What if you filled all of those roles *before* finding a partner or *outside* of your current partnership? Can you feel the sign of relief that automatically releases from the mere idea of that?

While the sacred masculine partner you just met in the previous section may not be "real," your nervous system doesn't know the difference between what's imaginary and what is real. If you allow yourself to believe that this person is your *partner*, and that they're just as real as a human man, you'll feel just as supported as if they were physically with you. But you have to *tend* to this relationship as if it is real—with prayer, love and devotion.

This next practice is going to serve you in honoring this partnership between you and your masculine as sacred.

- Find yourself a beautiful new ring. It doesn't matter if it's $5.00 or $5,000! Pick what makes you feel the most cherished as a bride.

- On a piece of paper, write down your vows as if you are speaking directly to your dream partner—the man who has met *every* one of your needs in love. The man who has shown up like nobody's business! How do you promise to love him? To be in devotion to him? To honor him? To remember him? Write them down.

- Tea-stain your paper so it looks like an old scroll! Not required, but highly recommended.

- Go somewhere in nature wearing something white, preferably a dress. You can go to a beach, the top of a mountain or a fairy-filled forest. If none of these places are available, simply go to a space where you feel a connection to — somewhere that feels sacred. Bonus: take a handful of rose quartz crystals (these stones hold healing properties for self-love and love with others) and create a circle around yourself with the crystals.

- At your destination, close your eyes, put a hand on your heart and connect with your sacred masculine partner. When you're ready, invite him into the circle and read your vows aloud. Once you've completed reading, give him space to speak to you. You may not hear any words, but notice if you have a particular *feeling* arise. Pay attention to anything that may occur as he has space to offer his love to you.

- Finally, place the ring on any finger that represents this marriage. It can be your actual ring finger, a middle finger or even a pinky. It doesn't matter which finger, so long as you feel ready to leave it on that particular finger.

- Close with a bow to seal in your sacred marriage.

Know that whenever the longing for love feels too intense, too painful and too uncomfortable, you can turn to your sacred masculine beloved to hold you close. Remember him. Remember your vows. Remember your devotion. Remember the artistry of your eternal love.

PART THREE: LIVING WITH YOUR SACRED MASCULINE

Depending on which archetype you want to embody, you can engage with your sacred masculine as that archetype.

When you're feeling sensual, dance in lacy garments for your sacred masculine.

When you're feeling playful, create a picnic for you and your sacred masculine to enjoy on the beach.

When you're feeling ceremonial, create a playlist of devotional music to share with your sacred masculine under a starry night sky.

When you're feeling loyal and in love, make a gift — such a crystal mandala or an engraved wooden box — and offer it to the spirit of your sacred masculine.

Treat this relationship as real, and watch how it *transforms* your relationship with earthly men. Here are some additional things you can do with your sacred masculine as regular practices:

1. Turn self-pleasure into pleasure with *him*. The next time you're feeling frisky, or you're looking for a quick sexual release, *slow down*. Instead of immediately grabbing a toy or turning on your laptop to watch porn, create a devotional space for you and your inner masculine. Touch your body the way you believe he would touch your body. Say things that you believe he would say. Talk to him. Offer him rose petals. Adorn your body with oil as if he was doing it. Additionally, you can close your eyes as you self-pleasure and imagine you're locking eyes with him. Feel his breath, feel his heartbeat, *feel him hold you*. If you do grab a toy, use it on you the way he would use it on you. If it's an internal toy, like a crystal dildo, let it move inside you as he would. This is how you can begin to train yourself to receive love and attention from actual partners on *this* deep of a level, before it's actually here. By doing this with your own sacred masculine, you can sovereignly choose to bring this level of intimacy into the bedroom with a real beloved.

2. Write love letters to him. Women have a lot of longing, and very

little places to put it! But guess who *loves* your longing? Your inner masculine. He eats that shit for breakfast! He finds it beautiful! He can't get enough! And the thing is—a lot of men love it too. Women just haven't yet grown accustomed to being honest and vulnerable with their own longing because of the stories they tell themselves about it being weak or stupid or needy. It's actually not—it's beautiful. And it's *such* a gift to witness the longing that pours out of a feminine being's heart. So, get yourself a journal to write love letters to your beloved. This will support you in validating your longing so that you can freely express it with a future partner when you miss him, inevitably delighting him in surprising unexpected ways!

3. Have conversations with him. When you feel out of sorts, tell him how he can serve you. Remember, *he is in service to YOU.* The masculine is here to protect, provide and support the feminine. When you begin to feel overwhelmed with your to do list and never-ending self-sufficiency, take a pause and tell him how he could support you. Can he command you to go take a nap? Can he command you to go to the spa and play hooky on work? Can he encourage you to go to a feminine embodiment practice to get outta your head and into your body? The masculine doesn't want to give you *more* to do—he wants to give you less! Let him take things off your plate by leading you into deeper states of rest and ease. By doing this with your inner masculine, you can start to get used to asking for support from a human man when the time is right. Get into the practice of asking for support *now* so that you can be vulnerable in those ways in partnership.

YOU GET WHAT YOU ARE

There's a popular theory in the personal development space that you don't just get what you want, you get what you are. When you embody the thing you want, you are an energetic match for it to come into your life. This couldn't be truer with the art of husbanding your feminine.

When you learn to guide, hold, embrace, lead, penetrate, and swoon your own feminine, not only do you *know* more clearly the kind of masculine partner you desire but you have incorporated this energy into yourself. It no longer lives outside of you. You are a complete, utter match for the level of consciousness you crave.

This practice isn't something you are doing willy-nilly. It's in deep devotion to the kind of partnership you're calling in — whether it's deepening the one you already have or preparing for a new one. The key to the relationship you crave lives within becoming it yourself.

WHEN ONE BECOMES TWO

In this past section, you've learned how to be an artist of love using arche-types, creativity, shadow work and monologues. You've learned some pretty badass psychology around your needs as a child and how they relate to your needs as an adult. You've also learned how to husband your own feminine and create a delicious, ongoing relationship to him, which is truly an act of devotion on your part to the health of *all* your future relationships.

By this point, you have all the tools required to start making art as all four of the artist of love archetypes in the comfort of your own room and heart. After all, as an artist of love, everything you create ultimately begins and ends with you. The relationship you have with yourself is the foundation of all creativity, and it is a relationship that requires meticulous attention day after day.

And, that said…you're probably wondering how this all actually relates *in a relationship*. You're probably intuiting, under the surface, that all of this can only go so far when you are alone and there's no, shall we say, co-star.

The truth is, you can only see and heal your patterns, habits, wounds, desires, longings, cravings and fears as far as you are willing to go. And that's not nearly as far as you can go when someone else's patterns, habits, wounds, desires, longings, cravings and fears are rubbing shoulders with yours.

The deepest spiritual practice you can have is to be in a relationship. Relationships will test you. They will open you. They will close you. They will teach you where you are not yet healed. They will show you where you're still looking for validation. They will highlight where you don't yet love yourself. They will show you how you collapse, how you make art, and how you are generous or selfish in love. Relationships will teach you what it means to be tender, fierce, desperate, caged, safe, free, erotic, triggered, pleasured, bored, sensitive, defensive and in love. They are a *mirror*.

To take off your shoes and willingly enter the temple of love, to kneel at the altar of relationship, to smell the incense of devotion and to pray at the feet of the Divine, day after day, is a sign of a true devotee...not to anyone outside of yourself, but rather, to love itself.

If you are ready for the next layer of the artistry of love, let's begin.

Part Three

THE ARTISTRY OF LOVE WITH OTHER

MADE FOR LOVING

You can go far in your healing journey with all of the solo tools available at your fingertips: talk therapy, feminine embodiment, psychology, hypnosis, tapping, crystal gridding, family constellations, boundary-setting, manifestation, kundalini breathwork, goat yoga, chanting, cold plunging, candle gazing, infrared red therapy, and all the Tony Robbins events your body can handle—but the *deepest* healing will happen in none other than relationship. *Romantic* relationship.

When we enter a relationship we willingly sign an invisible vow to be our partner's training arena for the great drama of life, and them, ours. When we dive into love, we are given all the opportunities we need in order to transform collapse into creativity, jealousy into generosity, insecurity into ingenuity, and selfishness into the sacredness.

And this should be really good news to you if you've got a feminine heart. Why? Cause you're *built* for love.

Even if you've got your own wounding, triggers or avoidant/anxious patterning, it doesn't stop you from being a woman. And deep within her core, Woman is made for love.

Woman is made for love because Woman *is* love.

She is made of silk sheets and red rosebuds. She is warm oil and foot massages. She is Indian Jasmine and African Frankincense. She is a late-night cuddle and an early morning breakfast in bed. She is the marriage vow and the ten-year anniversary. Anywhere there is a deepening of love, she can be found.

Whether you're invoking the Priestess, Oracle, Devotee or Enchantress, there is *one thing* they all have in common: they're all attuned to the flow of love, and they all have ways to amplify that love with their tools. So when love is flowing, you know how to amplify it and bring even more love. When love is *not* flowing, you know how to call it out and bring your love back into integrity.

As an artist of love, your gift of love-attunement can powerfully invite nothing but the absolute best from your relationship, calling your partnership into deeper integrity *as* a Priestess, Oracle, Enchantress or Devotee. Or as another character from a film or movie you're working with. How would Princess Leia bring her partnership back into the flow of love? Or Cruella de Ville? Or Hermione Granger? As an artist of love, you can find ways to deepen your relationship that are *creative*, even if it's born out of a conflict or challenge. It's half the fun!

When you *invite* your relationship into deeper, integral love as one of these archetypes, you can still remain in the feminine pole. One of the most magical things about the archetypes is that they are all embodiments of the feminine energy, and they all use their super-power of expression and love to *create* change rather than command or direct it.

To be clear, this is not mothering. Mothering is reverse polarity where you're in the masculine and your partner is in the feminine. Mothering is a kind of unsexy, hand-holding energy where you tell your partner what to do because you know best. Even though you may *think* mothering is the most nurturing thing you can do, it's actually the most emasculating. Nobody wants to rip clothes off when you're in the energy of mother and son, so please — stop telling your partner how to be a good boy for the sake of your sex life!

The feminine doesn't have any interest in *correcting*; she is more interested in embodying her truth no matter what and trusting the masculine will find his own way from receiving her expression. He is not her homework project. When the partnership gets out of alignment, she knows she can always steer herself in the direction life is asking her to go—with a powerful spine—knowing that her truth creates *transformation*.

In this section of the book, we will continue to explore how the archetypes create art, but this time in relationship.

THREE LEVELS OF RELATIONSHIP DEPTH

There are three types of relationship "depth" styles. Each one is important to understand because the depth of your relationship will play a big part in determining the depth of the art you make in it.

LIGHT AND FLUFFY

Some relationships are light and fairly fluffy. This couple keeps things on the surface, doesn't talk too much about their feelings and doesn't push each other's buttons.

The upside to a relationship like this is that you probably have a lot of fun together! You tend to fill the relationship with positive vibes over negative ones. You want to be each other's greatest cheerleaders, so you stick to highlighting all that's good about life rather than focusing on where things can be better. The connection is easy to maintain day-to-day due to its general friendliness.

The problem with this type of relationship is that it's usually surface-level only. Nothing deeper ever gets addressed, resolved, or even mentioned. And while that may seem like a good thing at first, over time it becomes a bigger and bigger problem. After the hundredth "my day was fine, how was yours?" convo, you start to ask yourself, "Do I *really* know this person?" When you want to inquire into their secretive personal mind, you hold back. When you feel a *complaint* bubble up, you repress it. You keep things calm and positive, because the idea of bursting your perfect relationship bubble is frankly frightening. And all the while you feel your energy slowly draining away as you fight to keep everything light and fluffy all the time.

A good relationship from television that demonstrates this dynamic is Dexter and Rita from the show *Dexter*. In case you don't know the show, Dexter is a serial killer who only kills bad people. Rita is his girlfriend, but she knows nothing about his secretive life as a killer because Dexter has kept it private. They have date nights together, play with Rita's kids, and talk about daily life. Everything seems fine for them. But there's a huge elephant in the room for the audience considering we know this massive secret that Rita doesn't. Dexter's serial killer hobby could serve as a really great metaphor for the light and fluffy couple—there's always stuff under the surface that is hungry to come out, but never does because nobody wants to disrupt the peace.

The truth is, it's those very secrets that are harming the relationship and blocking the flow of intimacy. This kind of relationship actually *needs* to allow a little more messiness and to expand its capacity to be with discomfort. In fact, the more comfortable you are with the messiness, the more intimacy will flow into your partnership. Messiness is where intimacy is created because it's *real*. Your longing, confusion, craziness and wildness are all treasures of your feminine heart, and they are all designed to inherently evoke more of the masculine from your partner as a rule of polarity. The deeper you go into energy, the deeper he will go into his consciousness. But again, allow the process to be messy—even the process of being messy. It's not always going to feel good, but that's exactly what your relationship may need in order to grow: more honesty.

BALANCED YET BORING

Some relationships are more harmonized between play and depth, meaning they encourage each other to share honestly and openly, but they're also down to spend their evenings together watching Netflix...maybe *too* many evenings.

This couple is comfortable in their routine. They may have had a spicy courtship, but once they began peeing with the door open, all mystique fell to the wayside. They no longer feel the need to "win" each other over.

If this is your relationship, you're probably finding that your polarity has suffered. As a woman, you may start wearing your retainer to bed even if there's a possibility of sex. You may stop shaving your legs, even though you feel much sexier when you do (no judgment to anyone who doesn't shave, so long as you feel empowered in it!). You may stop flirting with your beloved or making an effort to enchant him. Why bother if you've already got him?

An example from a movie that reminds me of this dynamic is Debbie and Pete in *This is 40*, played by Leslie Mann and Paul Rudd. The couple's polarity is drastically decreasing the older they get as more bills, responsibilities and stressors pile on them. The movie opens in the best way possible to demonstrate this—they're having sex in the shower of her 40th birthday and he ecstatically exclaims that he took Viagra. She angrily tells him to get off her and then they get into a debate about why he needs Viagra in the first place. The movie is a comedy, so while its job is to amplify all of the outrageous situations couples go through when they grow older together, it's also showing to us a clear demonstration of what happens when a couple doesn't prioritize their chemistry, polarity and artistry in love. And while that couple is married with two kids, this can happen to any couple, married or not.

Once again, the answer to this conundrum is to bring more artistry *into* the intimacy. This includes seducing, worshiping, praising, surprising and loving each other even amongst the pots and pans. This couple needs to prioritize space as well. This could be physical space where they take turns taking short trips without each other, or energetic space where they relieve their partner from having certain roles in the relationship from time to time, such as being each other's therapists. I'm not encouraging this couple to keep *secrets*, but rather, to allow some privacy. Your partner doesn't need to know each and every detail about your yeast infection, your friend's new apartment decoration or your favorite reality television show. Your partner also doesn't need to watch all of your favorite shows with you, or do everything you like to do.

While relationships require sameness, polarity requires *opposition*. The more alike you are, the more space you'll inherently need to keep the chemistry alive. If you resonate with this couple, look at all the ways you can trade zoning-out television time for perfectly good polarity-creating space. You can watch television in separate rooms, take solo getaways, or sleep in different beds a few nights per week. These are great, small ways you can incorporate space into your regular life to support re-enlivening chemistry.

BALLS TO THE WALL

And finally, we have the couple that likes to play full out—both in the highs as well as the lows. They are traversing spiritual, conscious and intimate territory together. They are here for all the gnarliest, deepest, and most beautiful experiences life has to offer with each other.

This couple has a natural polarity—one person is in the feminine and the other is in the masculine. She brings the energy and he brings the depth. This leads to incredible sex—the kind where it feels like she's being obliterated into a million pieces and he's being constantly reborn from the blinding beauty of her natural radiance. They are feeling god in their fuck—it's holy, surreal and beautifully heartbreaking.

And…

This same couple experiences a natural polarity in other places too—like their triggers. On the shadow level, this can lead to terrible, explosive fighting. This partnership lives for the extremes, and while they'd much rather be in the "love" extreme, it can be challenging to modulate the passion that bubbles up when either are upset.

A relationship from a television show that reminds me of this dynamic is Jessa and Adam from *Girls*, played by Jemima Kirk and Adam Driver. Adam and Jessa's love affair was extreme from the beginning, not only because they're both fiery humans, but because Adam was previously in a relationship with Jessa's best friend. They were having relations behind their friend's back, which inevitably added more sexual tension *and* passion to their romance.

In the final episode of season five, Jessa and Adam get into a massive argument and destroy the entire apartment, throwing every single thing in sight, until they end up breathing heavily after having sex on the glass-covered floor.

While not every relationship in this realm is physically violent or has record-breaking fights, sometimes the violence is all in the energy: sharpness of energy, loudness of voice, a closure of the heart, cruelty of words, threats of leaving the relationship, emotional withdrawing, unnecessary blaming, energetic collapse, accusatory behavior and unconscious manipulation.

To be clear, this does not automatically happen to every couple who wants to go deep, and this is certainly not the end result for every deep couple. This is merely a manifestation of unhealed trauma or unconscious shadow behavior.

The beautiful thing is, if you *are* with a partner who you would consider challenging in some way (energetically, spiritually, emotionally), your relationship is *deliciously ripe* for transformation.

You can find yourself in any three of these relationship dynamics across the span of your entire life. You may be balanced but boring with a long-term partner in your 20s but then balls to the wall with a short-term fling in your 30s. You can also experience all three dynamics throughout the course of *one* relationship, depending on different periods of growth you move through together. Think of these dynamics as seasons: each one offers both gifts and shadows, and you can alchemize all of them into deeper intimacy as a feminine artist of love.

FROM SHADOWS TO SAFETY

In their book *Getting the Love You Want*, Helen Hunt and Harville Hendrix present a revolutionary concept that may forever change how you view the challenges, shadows and conflicts that arise in your relationships.

The authors propose that adults find romantic partners who have both the *best* and *worst* qualities of their parents combined, so that they can (unconsciously) heal their original childhood wounds. This concept is related with what we talked about earlier in the book about core needs and wounds in partnership, but now we're looking at how this pattern has manifested itself in your romantic partnerships throughout your life, and how this can be a garden for fertile transformation.

Essentially, the unconscious does not understand the concept of time so it doesn't matter if you're five years old or fifty years old — the subconscious is *always* on the hunt to heal that initial childhood wound that your caregivers imprinted on you. The good news is that healing can also occur whether you're five or fifty — wounds can't tell time.

I'll use my client Madison as an example to demonstrate.

Madison always seemed to be in the wrong place at the wrong time as a kid, such as stepping into the kitchen to get a snack at the very moment her parents started a heated argument about money. Whenever this happened, her mother would get angry and yell at Madison for interrupting or being in the way. When Madison understandably reacted to this by panicking or crying, she would be scolded for her "insane emotional outbursts" and sent back to her room, snackless.

For the most part, Madison was a very happy-go-lucky kid, but anytime she felt even a small pang of sadness, she would feel completely taken over by the emotion, afraid mostly of what her emotions would do to her mother. If Madison's mother felt even a little bit embarrassed by Madison's outbursts, she would tell her to keep quiet, stop being so sensitive, and shut up.

At the same time, it was her mother who also adored her the most! Madison's mom bragged about Madison's excellence in school to all her friends, she took her out to ice cream after every ballet performance and she tucked her into bed each night with a story and a kiss.

So Madison never knew if she was going to get the side of her mother that kissed the ground she walked on or shut her down with a scold and a spanking. By the time she was in elementary school, Madison had already learned to present herself as good, quiet, reasonable, and palatable at all costs. For years, she made only choices that guaranteed *nobody* would be embarrassed because of her. Here are just a few results of those choices:

- Madison didn't set clear boundaries because of how threatened she would *feel* when she said "no." She didn't want to feel bad, uncomfortable or difficult, so she simply said yes to it all.

- Madison didn't show up with her friends fully as herself. There was a constant sensor in the back of her head running the show, questioning, "Is this too much?" "Will this make them uncomfortable?" "Should I speak up about that?" Being with friends was truly an exhausting experience, so she limited the amount of time dedicated to social activities.

- She didn't recognize or embody her gift as an Oracle because she didn't see her sensitivity as a superpower. Any intuition, inklings, or whispers from her heart were immediately shut down.

- She didn't have a connection with her own body, which led to repressed sexuality, vitality and radiance.

- Worst of all, she dated men who treated her just like her mother had—alternately adoring her and shaming her for her feelings. And instead of opening her heart and expressing anger, sadness, jealousy or any other emotion that would arise through *love*, she projected her inability to feel her feelings onto her partner. She was so uncomfortable with her own sadness, that she unconsciously directed it at her partners in a way that really was nearly abusive, just so that she could relive her initial childhood trauma, hoping for a new response.

Madison's story is not unique; every single human has something they did *not* receive in childhood and are currently searching for as an adult (while simultaneously pushing it away) and it's these core wounds and core needs that need your undivided attention.

When you find yourself in a partnership with someone who reminds you of the best and worst qualities of your caretakers you are most likely in what is called an *Imago Match*. This is another concept from *Getting The Love You Want*, and it means a couple that shows each other "unconscious images of familiar love." The couple reflects to each other a strikingly familiar image—one that they grew up seeing every day in their childhood.

These types of partnerships hold an incredible opportunity for deep, nervous-system healing, because if you're willing to do the work required, you're able to alchemize that original wound once and for all.

Once I clearly broke down the pattern Madison was re-entering over and over again, she started to see her addiction to the wound. For her, there was something familiar about being emotionally poked and prodded while simultaneously praised. It felt like home. And she realized she needed to create a new sense of home — the kind she *wished* she had grown up with.

During our coaching together, she began seeing a man named Luke. To be expected, he worshiped her from the start. He adored her hips, her hair, her laugh — he was smitten. From appearances alone, Madison carried a strong Playful Priestess code, so it wasn't hard for men to fall in love with what they saw on the outside.

Luke was kind, but he was also challenged by Madison's emotions. He didn't like her passive aggression, moodiness or sharpness so he would react defensively. He would get loud, judgmental and impatient. He would say things like, "Stop being so emotional." He really seemed like just another of the same men Madison kept attracting with her wound.

The difference was, now Madison had valuable information she could utilize in her partnership. The answer wasn't to dump Luke and move on — she'd done that with a dozen other guys and just kept repeating the same pattern with the next one.

Instead, she decided to use this relationship to practice feeling and her feelings and embracing the messiness in totality. Instead of projecting sadness, she could practice being sad. Instead of protecting her vulnerability, she could practice being vulnerable. Instead of shoving down her anger, she could practice being angry. Considering some of Luke's patterns felt like her mother's, she could use this opportunity to *create* the childhood she always wanted.

Overtime, Madison started finding creative ways to tell Luke when an emotion was coming up. She started simple: every time an emotion like insecurity popped up, she would clutch her heart and say, "My heart!" dramatically (like the Playful Priestess she loved to embody). Simply acknowledging the emotion gave it more permission to exist.

Overtime, she began to use other modalities in her toolkit such as dance, like the Erotic Enchantress. She began trading her old passive aggressive mind games for out-in-the-open, conscious playful sensuality. He loved when she combined her real insecurities (like being left) *with* her sensuality. It became a deeply erotic gift.

Madison and Luke's connection outgrew their reactive tendencies, and as a byproduct of *her* inner work, Luke's understanding and patience with emotions shifted drastically. She was vulnerable with him, and that realness allowed their intimacy and connection to deepen. Because *she* used their unique triggers as a pathway for healing, he grew to understand more about the emotional cycles of the feminine and why it's so important to be in service to a partner's feelings, not against them. They did major healing work together, and they've been in partnership ever since.

Relationships will serve your overall healing journey as a woman because they unveil your shadow aspects. They're designed to. You may see yourself as a perfectly sweet, charismatic, patient woman, but the minute your partner starts poking at your squishy, tender bits, your inner bitch comes out. Great, use that!

Some of the best art, ever, comes out of the shadow and your emotional triggers. We've been speaking about "alchemy" throughout this book, and I want to highlight that using triggers to create art is a pristine example of alchemical magic. You can turn something karmic into something dharmic. You take a wound that would traditionally lead you to closing your heart, and instead open into greater liberation through being creative with it. You don't have to keep pretending like an argument never happened, you can milk it for all its worth to create art like an artist of love archetype would! Write a poem of passion, film a video, create a game, build a temple of truth — *create*. Not only will this *validate* and *free* your shadow into deeper liberation, but it will be in service of deepening intimacy with your beloved and your innermost child self.

TURNING DRAMA
INTO DHARMA

Richard Rudd, author of *The Gene Keys*, proposed that where there is drama, there is dharma. Dharma is a term that refers to one's sacred duty, divine assignment in this life, or reason for being here.

The idea of turning one's drama (the closed-hearted kind, not the Playful Priestess kind) into dharma means that the relationship bringing up your deepest fears (abandonment, being smothered, betrayal, being controlled, feeling stuck, take your pick) can also serve you in manifesting your dharma. Your biggest purpose in life! Your entire reason for being here!

For example, one of my deepest childhood struggles was feeling like my expression was not welcome. I was raised in the south, where being a woman was, on its own, a loaded subject constantly up for debate, usually by the men in the church. There were all sorts of rules about how women were supposed to behave, dress and act. It was—and is—a chronic issue that stems from the mentality that women are property and should act in ways that men appreciate.

I've since made my entire life about expression, from what I teach in my work, to how I date, to how I live my life alone. But OF COURSE I have been in relationships with men, over and over, who feel challenged by my expression. And in these relationships, I still get sharp instead of vulnerable. I still get withdrawn instead of open. I still collapse instead of create. It's normal. This stuff runs *deep*.

That said, I constantly use these challenging moments in relationships *as* a gateway for art. That's the incredible thing about these drama-dharma connections: every conflict is an opportunity to be creative.

The deeper the trigger and childhood pain, the higher possibility you have to transform those fears into love in your relationship and with your partner. You can become the caregivers you never had. You can learn to cherish, protect, and hold each other in such a way that heals the nervous system and imprints rich, nourishing love.

Triggers happen in every relationship. Some may be on a larger and more frequent scale, but there is *no* relationship on earth that goes without conflict, frustration and momentary head-butting. These conflicts are fabulous news to an artist of love because they allow you to make a decision — you can either collapse at the challenge, slamming the door and shutting down, or *expand, open* and *train your body to rise through the trigger.*

If you open through triggers in love, you can quite literally train your nervous system to be able to meet and receive more conflict in all of life. And your ability to alchemize pain into purpose will not be limited to only your romantic relationship…it will affect every area of your life.

For example, if something frustrating happens at work, you'll know how to bring the conflict to the surface so that there's an opportunity for connection amongst you and your co-workers. Maybe something awkward happens with a friend, like they don't reply to a text for a few days, and it hurts your feelings. You won't just shove it down in secrecy, you'll create a little piece of art to reveal your heart while also being vulnerable. You'll be able to joke with that great aunt who always comments on your weight at family gatherings in a way that's playful, but not pissy. You can enlighten people on how to enter greater depths of intimacy without closing your heart off in the process.

So, what does it look like to create art in the context of a relationship?

Similar to what we explored in the previous section about being an artist of love with yourself, being an artist of love with other is also about alchemizing water into wine — but now, you're doing it as an offering. You're creating art not *only* for yourself, but also for the health of your relationship's ecosystem. You're creating art to liberate deeper love for both of you.

VERONICA

Veronica, a student of mine, was an intuitive, sensitive woman who had a deep connection with the spirit realm. She was the kind of woman who wore her heart on her sleeve, loved deeply, grieved openly and did everything in the name of love. Veronica was in a relationship with a man named Kyle — if she was classical jazz, Kyle was heavy metal. Kyle was loud, opinionated and bold.

As you can imagine, Veronica and Kyle had a natural, effortless polarity. They were on opposite ends of the spectrum: her softness was a match for his strength just like his passion was a match for her ease. This made for an excellent sex life.

Unconsciously, they attracted each other because they wanted a piece of what the other had. They recognized the unintegrated qualities that they *wanted* to have themselves. She wanted a slice of his confidence and guts, and he wanted a slice of her delicacy and grace.

Oftentimes it's those very qualities we find attractive in our partner that drive us nuts when we're triggered. Veronica and Kyle would have a nice quiet dinner, but after a small blip in communication, his voice would raise, she would shut down and both of their walls would spike up. Because she hadn't yet integrated her own confidence and grandiose energy, she felt afraid in the presence of his (when he was upset). Because he hadn't yet integrated his own intuitive sensitivity (due to years of having it shamed out of him), he couldn't empathize with her freeze response.

So what happens in moments like this?

You either continue to collapse… *or*…

You turn drama… into dharma! You turn triggers…into masterful pieces of art!

Since Veronica most deeply related to the Erotic Enchantress, we worked together to explore ways she could empower herself to use her energy of eroticism and her strategy of dance to (1) liberate her own stuck expression and (2) make an offering to Kyle that would open his heart (while still making a point).

She wanted to send him a video, so together we looked at what message she wanted him to get from watching it, as well as what she intended for him to *feel* from it. She told me she wanted him to understand that she's sensitive, and it's painful for her to have to stretch to meet him in his energy, and she would love to trust that he can remain calm to work through something. She wanted him to feel, from watching this video, that she loves him, and she's not going anywhere. She wanted him to feel her devotion.

Veronica began filming a sacred strip tease. She filmed a few versions of it, but every time she began to cry. She was touching a deeper and more emotion: longing.

So, as the creative being she was, she decided to use what was coming up and she put on the song "Love Me Tender" by Elvis Presley. She danced *incredibly slow* in front of the camera, just with a thin slip on, revealing through her eyes the longing she was feeling.

She sent him a text, "Can I show you something?"

He wrote back, "Yes."

She sent him the video, and he called her within minutes to say, "Baby, this was so beautiful. Thank you for sharing your heart. I love you and I want to be able to hold you better. Can we sit down tomorrow with Kelly (their therapist) and talk about this?"

There are two things to note about Veronica's offering.

Firstly, she started with her original design as an Erotic Enchantress, but let herself freestyle based on what felt the most *true*. Let your art shape shift. You may start to create one thing and end up somewhere totally different. That's the beauty of it!

Secondly, she didn't over explain the video to him before sending it—she merely asked if she could show him something. I told her to ask him first, simply because this creates a permission field for the art to enter, which is a key component to being an artist of love with others. You're not asking them permission to be yourself—you're asking them if they're ready to *receive*. It sets both of you up for success if you give an offering when your partner gives a green light for receiving it.

If she had said, "Hey, I want to send you something, but you have to promise not to laugh, and the point of it is to make your heart open and I don't know if I did the best quality of filming but…" and so on, the actual transmission of the art would be manipulated.

You want to let your art land however it may. If your beloved doesn't quite understand what you're trying to say, they will let you know.

Veronica and Kyle ended up growing in love over the course of the next year, thanks to *her* consistent artistry. The more she revealed her heart to him in these creative ways, the more *he* sharpened up and led them into being a better couple (like immediately getting a therapy session in the books). Her heart inspired his leadership. Her energy inspired his depth.

He may have not been making dancing videos back (and would you really want that?), but it did turn the keys of his engine and get him thinking about ways he could provide the support Veronica and their relationship needed.

10 THINGS I HATE ABOUT YOU

One of my favorite film examples of turning a relationship trigger into art comes from the classic 90s film *10 Things I Hate About You* (which is a modern version of Shakespeare's *The Taming of the Shrew*).

In it, Julia Stiles plays Kat (a perfect example of a feminine being who masquerades as a masculine one) and Heath Ledger plays Patrick (a masculine being with a bad boy edge). Patrick is enlisted to win Kat's heart so that his friend can take Kat's sister out on a date (Kat's dad has a rule that his younger daughter can only go on a date if Kat goes too).

Over the course of the film, Kat eventually falls in love with Patrick, and Patrick falls equally in love with Kat. She tragically finds out the secret that their romance was an entire setup and ends up devastated, humiliated and bitter.

At the end of the film, Kat and Patrick are in a class together and it's time for the students to read their class projects out loud. Kat volunteers to go first, walks to the head of the class and begins reading her poem, which is about ten things she hates about Patrick. She doesn't say his name, but he knows the ten things she hates are specifically about him. She begins to cry as she finishes her poem and makes eye contact with Patrick as she runs out of the room.

This is a perfect example of *creativity in love*. Being creative in love isn't always about making playful, erotic or sexy pieces of art — sometimes it's about meeting the most vulnerable, tender parts of our hearts and opening through them while *also* revealing our disgust, pain or resentment.

For the record, I imagine Kat is a Sacred Devotee. Reading a poem for all to hear at the front of the class is definitely a devotional and courageous act of love. (And, spoiler alert if you haven't seen the movie, Patrick responds to this act of devotion by meeting Kat at her car with a meaningful gesture of his own, and they end the movie getting back together.)

Kat accomplished four things with the brave sharing of this poem:

1. **She revealed a painful truth with an open heart.** Kat gives a perfect example of what it looks like to share your heart without shame or blame. Making art is about expressing—not projecting. It doesn't need to go "into" anybody else—just up and through you.

2. **She opened the moment to more love by revealing said truth.** Intimacy flourishes where there's honesty! Stop waiting for the other person to do something in order for you to free your self-expression. How about you do it *now* simply because there is no other way for you to exist? If you finally stop waiting, you will be mesmerized by how much love you are able to create.

3. **She offered him a gift.** In fact, she offered the entire class a gift—and the entire world who has seen the film! When we create art out of our emotions and offer it to our partner, we are giving a gift to *anyone* it may affect…free of charge and without any attachment.

4. **She healed a part of her own nervous system by creating something out of her pain and being witnessed in it.** The part of her body that says, "No I can't expose *that* part of myself, or I'll no longer be the badass tough girl I am!" was shifted at that moment—at least a little. Not only because she expressed herself, but also because there were witnesses. Something magical happens when we allow ourselves to be seen in the parts we normally hide.

Even though it feels like you're offering yourself up as a human sacrifice whenever you reveal the most tender parts of yourself, you're simply returning back home to the most natural place your body knows. *Love.*

In *Finding God Through Sex*, David Deida writes, "Because love is inde-structible, you don't need to protect yourself." An open heart doesn't require twenty pounds of armor. Opening the heart brings more healing, as long as you remember you're opening and surrendering into the oceanic love of the Great Divine.

THE ARCHETYPES
IN RELATIONSHIP

Now that we've gone through a few examples, let's explore how each archetype might create art in a partnership. You can choose to embody any one of these, at any given time, based on the energy you intuit your relationship needs.

LOYAL ORACLE

When in a relationship, the Loyal Oracle liberates love by exposing her vulnerability and deepest truth. She lets her longing flow up her spine and out through her eyes. She summons the fire from her pussy and sends it out through her voice.

One of my students, Kimmy, had a tremendous capacity for compassion and would often guard it with a passive aggressive exterior. She didn't want to feel all the tenderness and understanding that was hidden within, because if she did, she feared she would be taken advantage of.

Her partner, Jamie, often felt misunderstood and "shut out" during their fights. It would normally go like this: he would say something off the cuff, she would feel hurt and reply in a snooty not-herself-way, he would feel frustrated and defensive, and she would shut down.

One day, stepping fully into the Loyal Oracle, she promised herself she would be fully devoted to revealing her raw heart the entire day. When she saw the strawberries in the fridge were turning moldy, she stuck out her tongue and said, "*Yuckkkk!*" When her assistant said she had a dentist appointment on Thursday, she gave a loud deep belly groan (which made them both laugh). When she stubbed her toe on her coffee table she chose not to silence her yelp and instead chose to show her living room furniture *exactly* how painful that stub was by yelling, crying and rolling on the floor.

At dinner, when she was in the kitchen, Jamie made a comment about her actually doing her archetype homework. He said, "Wow, I can't believe you were actually able to do it."

This is a comment that would normally lead to her to collapse in some way—perhaps slam the door, make a pissy reply, or project her pain back onto him to make him feel sad instead, but this time she stepped into her truth as a Loyal Oracle.

Continuing the raw heart exercise, Kimmy clutched her heart, looked Kyle in the eyes, and softly said, "Ouch." In that one word, she put all of the hurt she was feeling.

Jamie immediately came and hugged her. He said, "Oh baby, I'm sorry, that's not what I meant. You always do what you say you'll do."

Kimmy's response was so simple, yet effective, because there's no story connected to it. She wasn't saying, "Ouch—that hurts and you *always* hurt me, and you *love to* win in arguments and I'll *never* be good enough for you."

She only said, "Ouch."

The feeling is much more authentic than the story.

Why do this? Why reveal in such a way?

Because your truth is important. It is *needed* in your relationship. Every time you speak up or reveal your raw heart, you are protecting your love from unwanted energies such as resentment, bitterness and blame.

It's also worth noting that revealing isn't something you do to "get" something. It is an offering of your truth. And the irony is, the more you allow your feelings to be an offering, rather than a clenchy pursuit to make your partner change, the more effective it is for your partner's own heart to open wider and feel you better.

PLAYFUL PRIESTESS

There's nothing worse to a Playful Priestess than feeling like the part of her who is youthful is not welcome in a relationship. Maybe she feels self-conscious that this part of her is too much, too young, too silly, too loud or too insensitive. The incredible thing about the Playful Priestess archetype is that it's quite the opposite—she has a unique gift for bringing in levity whenever levity is needed.

"Comic relief" is an amusing moment with the sheer purpose of breaking up all the serious shit in a play or scene; it provides temporary relief from all the tragedy at bay.

A Playful Priestess working on her craft knows the importance of learning how to decipher when and where play is needed versus when to relax into the seriousness. She's agile like that—she knows how to be with the current moment, while also being with the possibility of something a bit more sparkly and beautiful.

Sarah absolutely hated the monotony of online dating. Swipe left, swipe right, creatively find out if they have a car / a good job, if they have kids yet, if they're a smoker, if they're taller than her, and then maybe, just maybe, go out on a date (after hemming and hawing about who chooses the place).

Being that Playful Priestesses are a mirror for their environment, she took it to heart that she was hating this process. If she was dreading the humdrummery of it all, it most likely needed a playful facelift.

As if she was Tinkerbell getting spanked, Sarah drizzled a little of her glitter over the process and decided to view online dating as a feminine embodiment practice. How much could she be in her fullness? Energy? Light? Light? Emotion? Each person she swiped right on, she declared, would be a polarity practice partner. The more she entered her feminine, the more they would (as a natural byproduct) enter the masculine.

With her next match, Viktor, she started their conversation (yes, a feminine being can also take initiative) with a classic playful question: "Truth or Dare?"

VIKTOR: Oh, definitely a dare.

SARAH: Excellent choice, kind sir. I dare you to read me your favorite erotic poem in your best British accent. But, like, slowlyyy.

It took him a few hours, but he came back with gusto, leaving a beautiful audio note of himself reading a poem called "At the Touch of You" by Witter Bynner. Staying with the theme of femininity, she revealed how that made her feel with a steady stream of bright emojis (heart eyes, a pink flower, a clap, the gold sparkle, kitty cat kiss) and an audio note of her own saying, "Ahhhh, I loved that. Thank you, thank you!"

While Sarah and Viktor didn't end up getting married, they did go on several dates — each one serving as an opportunity for her to bring her energy, playfulness and spirit. Not only was her experience with Viktor a playground for her highest embodiment, but every date was.

She amplified her food moan when she bit into her first delicious bite of sushi, she texted him heart-eye emojis after their first date, she went all in with her outfits and adornments, and she even sent him a video of her dancing by the ocean because she wanted to offer him the gift of her mermaid expression.

What if you used dating as an experience to play and actually have fun? To remember that life is a big party? To dress in bright colors, drink bubbly libations and sing at the top of your lungs? To celebrate each connection even *if* the guy you're on a date with probably won't be your forever partner? To gift the person in front of you with joy even if they're not loving you precisely the way you want?

Dating is your best friend when it comes to embodying the Playful Priestess because very few situations in life offer moments of togetherness *without* a back story attached yet. If you're new to dating each other, you don't have any history. The soil is fertile. You can be anyone you want. There's nothing to lose.

If this person is your long-time partner, can you let each date be a fresh start? A new moment to inspire yourself and your beloved into remembering why life is worth living? To bless his path with your open heart, shimmering eyes and bountiful smile? Dating as a Playful Priestess renews the inherent vitality of life because she reminds us what we're really here to do: experience bliss.

EROTIC ENCHANTRESS

The Erotic Enchantress is a true blessing in a relationship because her entire body can feel when the polarity is slipping through the cracks. It's like nails on a chalkboard. Therefore, she is naturally inclined to do what is necessary to create a little distance so that the "pounce factor" remains on the up and up.

(The "pounce factor" is a term a former boyfriend taught me. It is an imaginary scale to determine how much you want to jump someone's bones at any given moment.)

While growing as a couple comes with familiarizing yourself with the humanness of each other, the Erotic Enchantress is very careful to keep some aspects of her life private—for the sake of polarity.

She's intentional about how often she talks about exes, she keeps a separate bathroom, she takes solo trips and she doesn't tell her partner *everything* going on in her mind. Though relationships need sameness in order to work, polarity needs opposition. Sometimes that polarity is natural, like a male versus a female, and sometimes it must be created, like taking intentional space.

My client Sasha and her beloved, Michael, have a deep care for each other's hearts and are taking their "caretaking" role seriously. They go to therapy, have honest communication and feel safe with each other in all regards. But…the interesting (and completely normal) phenomenon they were experiencing is that the safer their love was and the more time they spent together, the lower their pounce factor became!

That's because they have the "sameness" piece down, but they're not excelling in the "opposition" component. They need more distance, which can be created either physically or energetically. The art of creating energetic opposition (while even remaining in the same room) *is* the art of polarity.

One day Sasha wanted to embrace her version of the Erotic Enchantress and let her pussy lead. She was hungry to feel their pounce factor rise, and she made it her sacred mission to do so.

Sasha put on her black leather harness underneath a sundress and turned on the sound system. Michael was sitting on their couch with his headphones in, working on something for his startup.

Without asking Michael to do anything, Sasha started dancing to the music she turned on. In her own world, she danced, as she widened her awareness to feel him watching her. Eventually he took off his headphones and started to enter the world she was creating at that moment.

Sasha slowly, ever so slowly, made eye-contact with him and showed, through her eyes, the longing she was feeling for him. Even if their pounce factor wasn't sky high, she could still feel her erotic hunger because of her *own* connection to her pussy. She didn't need him to do anything—her eroticism was hers and hers alone.

So Michael continued to witness as Sasha blinked with lust and teasingly stripped off her dress to the music. Absorbed in her light and radiance, he began to breathe deeper, grounding the moment. The deeper he breathed, the safer she felt to open and reveal.

Within a few moments, they were taking off each other's clothes and rolling on the living room floor together. The pounce factor was back.

Polarity doesn't need to be understood by both people in order to work: it just takes one, very determined, practitioner. When Sasha declared in her head that she was going to embody her archetype, the practice already began.

If you notice that the safer and healthier your relationship becomes, the less sexy it feels, you are right on track. This is normal and it's *not* a sign that your partner isn't "the one." It's merely a sign that *your* practice is needed. Get to it, Enchantress.

SACRED DEVOTEE

The Sacred Devotee doesn't *do* lazy. Everything she does is connected to the sacred. When she watches Netflix, it's with intentionality. When she makes love, it's in connection to Divinity. When she eats her food, it's with prayer and gratitude. When she takes a walk, it's an immersion with nature. There is meaning in everything for the Sacred Devotee.

In partnership, the Sacred Devotee knows how to turn a regular ole fight into an opportunity for depth and devotion. She can use a trigger to create a magical moment, symbolizing a renewed sense of commitment as a couple. As if she is a character in a great drama, she will create the perfect backdrop, set the ideal scene and tend to all five senses with detail.

About seven months into a past relationship, my partner (let's call him Ken) and I had a gut-wrenching fight that left both of us feeling scared to trust each other. We were a classic balls to the wall couple where our highs were super-duper high and our lows were super fucking low. That said, we were committed to creating safety and equilibrium for each other even when we felt unseen, unheard and frustrated.

After this particular fight, as the Sacred Devotee I am, I told him I wanted us to create a re-commitment ceremony to each other—but not just the *idea* of the person in front of us, but also the *reality* of the person. I wanted us to recommit to the flesh and bone, triggers and traumas, pain points and panic buttons of each other and to hold those crunchy, sticky parts as sacred—not just the parts that glow and radiate. *All of it is sacred.*

Though my archetypes are not for men, I can almost guarantee that Ken would also resonate the most with the Sacred Devotee archetype as ceremony was his lifeblood. Together, we created a ceremony specifically in devotion to our recommitment.

There were several components to this specific ceremony. First, we spent the morning writing our vows to each other—nine in total, as nine is a holy number. I ordered special tea-stained scroll paper and hand-dyed ribbons so we could make our vows look like actual scrolls.

During the evening, we created a sacred space together. This included piling up sheepskins, lighting candles, turning on the fireplace, dimming the lights, cleansing the room with sage, and setting up two meditation cushions to face each other.

Lastly, we separated to prepare our holiest of temples—our bodies. Before any kind of ceremony (including making love), Ken and I would bathe or shower and get ready for the ceremony. I would normally take a bath, adorn my body with luxurious oils and apply a little bit of makeup. Nothing over the top, but enough to take care of myself.

For this particular ceremony, we both wore white (we didn't even tell each other we were going to do so — it just happened).

The ceremony itself had several components. We had a sensory ritual, where we took each other in through the five senses (touch, taste, sound, smell, sight), followed by a traditional hand-fastening ceremony (binding our hands together in love) and then reading vows to each other under the romantic light of a flickering candle.

By the end of the ceremony, we were in a trance-like love state, each yearning to be filled by the other. Him with my radiance and surrender, me with his presence and penetration.

Our ceremony was a divinely sacred way to recommit to our love and devotion for each other.

As the Sacred Devotee archetype, you can harness the power of ceremony to profoundly deepen your partnership at *any* stage of your love. Whether it's your third date, third month, third year or thirtieth anniversary, there are small and big ways you can symbolically honor your love.

You can return to the location you first met and read each other love poems, you can eye gaze with each morning for five minutes, you can sit in yab-yum (women in the lap of man, with legs wrapped around his waist) and breath in unison, you can create fertility rituals before embarking to conceive, and/or you can have Tea ceremony each Saturday under the morning sun.

Ceremony is a way of life — just like artistry. All it takes is one person (you, my love) to prioritize it.

CREATING ART IN PARTNERSHIP

Your turn. Think about something you have been experiencing in your own relationship (or if you're single, something you've experienced in the past) that may have been a sticky point for you. Feel the feelings that come up with that frustration, or memory, and allow yourself to imagine freely: what *creativity* wants to come through this?

Here are some other questions you can explore in your journal as you create your own work of art.

* What are some behaviors from your beloved that trigger you or have triggered you in the past? Write a couple of them down.

* Which archetype currently feels the most enticing and liberating? Write down her artistic flavor and creative strategy.

* How could you bring some artistry and creativity into the trigger to liberate more love? List three ideas here, then choose the one that speaks to you most strongly.

* Great! Now, what embellishments could you add to that idea to take it to the next level? *Costumes? Music? Sparkles? Confetti? Blindfolds? Boom boxes? Flying tomatoes?*

Now get started, you little Mistress of Creativity! You got some art to make.

ACTING: A PRACTICE FIELD FOR PARTNERSHIP

A question I often receive from people is, "But HOW do I make art out of my triggers in the moment when I'm so damn triggered!! How can I invoke the Erotic Enchantress or Playful Priestess when all I want to do (and feel like I *can* do) is slam the door?"

The answer is simple: practice this as a lifestyle when you're *not* triggered so that you've developed the muscle for when you are.

In the last section we looked at how monologues can help you create a relationship with your shadow sides so that you have autonomy over your own emotions. The monologue is a practice that you *do* until it becomes something you *are*. The practice of feeling and embodying the nutrient that the monologue offers, eventually leads to having that nutrient integrated.

When becoming an artist of love with other, your acting practice moves from monologues to partnered scene work. Having scene work, where you act scenes with another, creates a container for expressing, emoting and revealing in new ways, so that you can eventually integrate those new ways into partnership. That way, you'll have trained this artist's muscle within your creative psyche and can use it regardless of whether you're triggered or calm as a cucumber.

SCENE WORK MAKES THE DREAM WORK

You are an actor of your own life. Every day you interact with other humans, you are in a *scene.* Every time you come together with your beloved, you are co-creating the unfurling moment, leading each other from one place to the next. Every move *you* make dictates the move *they* will make.

Scene work is a practice ground for relationships. It will help you become a better girlfriend, wife and partner because it will show you all the ways you hold back, tighten up and ultimately restrict the flow of intimacy, and support you in unraveling those tendencies. Ultimately, acting is an embodiment practice. It will teach you how to get back into the body and to feel your feelings like the liberated feminine being you are, especially in relationships.

Great actors memorize their lines but leave ample room for *how* they're said. This is because a scene between two people builds in the back-and-forth exchange of lines. The way one actor exclaims something with absolute *joy* versus saying the exact same thing with fire-burning *hatred* will determine the way the other actor speaks in response.

When actors are locked into the way they think they need to feel or the way they need to speak, the entire scene will feel fake and forced. These actors are not fully present. They're waiting to deliver their next line and completely missing the body language, tone and emotion in their scene partner.

On the other hand, the actors who are fully in the present catch all of these little details that illuminate what their scene partner is feeling, such as tone shifts, expressions, accentuations, body language and pauses with meaning. These little moments are where the scene happens.

MOVING BEYOND THE BACKSTORY

In 2019, I was in a short film called *Falling Short* where I played a flirtatious woman named Steph who was in a love triangle with a couple old friends from high school. In order to feel Steph as not just a character, but as a real woman with her own struggles, desires and yearnings, my acting mentor had me sit down and write an entire backstory for my personal knowledge of her. When an actor knows their character's backstory, which leads to knowing what their character *wants* in life, their relationship to them deepens. It's subtle, but it's important. If their character is just a name on a script, they won't have any apparent overlap between them and the character. If they're personified and have real emotions like grief, longing, confusion or desperation, the actor can connect with them on a real-life level.

Letting my imagination run wild, I decided that Steph was a Scorpio with an alcoholic father and an absent-minded mother. She was a pharmaceuticals sales representative who spent way too much time out at the bars, and too little time nourishing her long-standing friendships. Steph was sensitive, but deep down, she felt like a fake and a phony, as all she ever really wanted was to know she was worthy of love from her parents.

In one of the final scenes, Steph and her three friends Ross, Jess and Bobby were nonchalantly playing spin the bottle. Ross was eyeing Jess a little too much for Steph's liking, and she was starting to feel insecure that he was more interested in Jess than in her. Jess and Bobby decide to go home early and left Ross and Steph in the kitchen with an awkward empty bottle.

Even though we didn't have any lines left, my scene partner decided to improvise and drunkenly brought the bottle to his lips and said to me, "We can keep playing," with a slur and wink.

I was legitimately caught off guard and started laughing. But once I realized I was laughing, I thought, *ugh no! Steph would not laugh! She's insecure! I've got to keep a straight face.* I sobered up my laugh and pulled it together in time to end the scene with a somber, "No, I don't want to keep playing."

The director called *cut* and my scene partner said, "That was the best take you've done yet. Your laugh was great…it was real. Don't stop that next time—let it keep going. Don't get in your own way."

In that moment, I had manipulated the scene in order to get the result I wanted, but I actually stopped the flow of connection by shutting down what was really happening and forcing something else. I was embarrassed that I was being a bad actor by letting the "Madelyn" version of my character get in the way, so I abandoned the moment with Ross in order to follow the thread of my backstory.

The thing about backstories is that they live in the body—in both real life and in scene work. Your backstory as a woman is very similar to your backstory as an actor: your body already knows it, so your mind doesn't have to. In fact, the more your mind holds onto your story, the less present you are with the current moment. If you keep trying to remember the backstory you have created (for your character or for your real-life self), every single choice you make will come from *thinking* you way through your life, rather than feeling your way through.

In both scene work and relationship work, the key is to trust the innate intelligence of your body. Your body remembers without having to think. Trust it knows something in a way that the mind can't, and you don't need to have that all figured out in order to respond to what's in front of you. The whole practice is to stop *forcing* and to simply be with what is.

My fellow actors and I ran the scene again (over thirty times in total), and each time I made it my mission to just be a little more present with what was there, rather than what I wanted to be there. I put my focus in the moment, and stripped away any thought about how I "should" respond. I let *Madelyn* meet *Steph* in every scene. We ended up getting many vulnerable real moments and I let my reactions come out more and more naturally every time.

OVERCOMING FEAR OF YOUR (ACTING) PARTNERSHIP

There may be a few reasons why you may be afraid to act with a scene partner, such as:

- It's hard to memorize lines while also interacting with someone else.

- You don't like the sound of your voice.

- You're going to mess up and this other person will see it, so why risk the embarrassment?

- It feels vulnerable to practice an intimate scene with someone who's not a romantic partner.

- You don't know how or where to find a partner.

- You don't have time or bandwidth to deal with the logistics of rehearsing with another person.

These are all perfectly valid reasons, and yet they are ALL reasons to do it anyway. Your relationship to this practice can be a mirror for your relationship to love. How often do you hold back from bringing your artistry into love because you're not going to do it perfectly? How often do you not do the thoughtful idea you had for your beloved because you don't have the time?

How often do you not take a risk in love because you don't want to embarrass yourself? How often do you avert your eyes from a platonic friend because you don't want to create a moment that feels intimate and deep?

Scene work will teach you how to be an artist of love because it will teach you to make creative choices. This works the same way monologues did! You will want to try your scenes with more mystique or sadness or elation or frustration, like you're drunk, just got a promotion, are ten days late on a mortgage, or have a spider in your pants. There are so many imaginary circumstances you can *add* to the scene to infuse it with a different energy, just like you can as an artist of love.

Throughout this book, we've been discussing the importance of range—and of exploring the thousands of women in your one body. Acting is a way you get to explore these parts of yourself, and acting with a *partner* is how you get to bring these parts of yourself into connection with others.

PRACTICE: SCENE WORK

Scene work is not meant to be perfect. In fact, there is no objective goal—the practice of performing a scene *is* the end result. Let it be a fun exploration of different aspects of yourself as a woman. Practice the art of instinct! Let yourself improvise with the lines! Make different choices and surprise your partner! And please, since you're not auditioning for a Spielberg movie, don't stress about memorizing the lines perfectly. This is more about being in your body than being in your head, so if memorization stresses you out, give yourself the space you need to let it be messy.

- Ask a friend, classmate, coach, family member or your beloved if they'd like to do scene work with you. You definitely don't *have* to do scene work with a romantic partner, but you certainly can if that feels inspiring for you both. Alternatively, if you don't want to ask any friends, or they're not available, you can find a private acting coach or go to a local acting class. You'll learn stronger techniques this way, and meet other potential scene friends!

- Find a script you want to work with. There are hundreds online, but you can also order a screenplay from Amazon, or even write down a scene line-by-line from your favorite movie. I would recommend starting with something about 5-6 pages in length.

- Together with your partner, write down the who, what, when, where, and why of both your characters. Who are they? What do they want in the scene? When is the scene taking place? Where are they? Why are they there? Why do they want what they want?

- Okay great, now that you know all of that, let it go. Remember the backstory in your body, but don't let your mind dwell on it.

- Begin to rehearse your lines together *without* any specific tones, accentuations, attitude, etc. Just rehearse it boring and plain. As *little* personality as possible.

- Once your lines are even slightly memorized, you can begin to add tone into the script. Pay particular attention to what your *scene* partner is doing, and let yourself react as authentically as possible to their lines and *how* they same them.

- Begin to make creative choices, based on imaginary circumstances. For example, how would you say your lines *now* if…

  » You secretly have a crush on your scene partner but you can't make a move because it's against HR policy at your place of work.

  » You have to file for bankruptcy because you're broke as a joke and need to tell your partner.

» You just received three orgasms from Timothée Chalamet and want to dish out the juicy gossip to your scene partner.

» Your husband is an FBI agent investigating your scene partner for a possible crime but your scene partner doesn't know.

Come up with as many scenarios as you'd like with the same script. Allow yourself to meet each run-through of the script with freshness, as if you've never said these words before.

Once you've worked through your first scene or two, start to notice how your responsiveness in scene work may be transferring over into your real life. Are you feeling more present with your partner? Are you starting to become more expressive? Are you reacting to life with a little more gusto? Are you aware of your feelings a bit more easily? What shifts are you noticing?

The more you do this work, the more transparent you'll become in your feelings, thoughts and desires with a beloved. You will feel a "portal" open in yourself. Whereas before you may have not had a desire, all of a sudden you'll have many! Whereas before you may have not been sensitive to a time away from your beloved, you may yearn for them in a way you never did before! Whereas previously you may have been totally content with your routine together, you may want more spice, adventure and spontaneity. You're *becoming* more, so you're *wanting* more.

When your portal of feminine expression opens up, you feel things more deeply. I encourage you to be honest, open and *real* with the stuff that comes up. Investigate it on your own and see what you want to do with it. Do you want to bring it to your beloved? Dance with it? Emote it? Embody it? Infuse it? Don't make it a problem to fix, by any means, because there's nothing to fix! Instead, make it a new adventure to dive into. Use your feminine heart as a compass for where the relationship is to go next.

Remember, energy *is* the feminine. When you practice feeling emotions and responsiveness in scenes, you are engaging in feminine embodiment practice. This is an incredibly fun and beautiful way to practice exploring and meeting the thousands of different women all living inside your one body…and then bringing them to your relationship.

SAVED BY THE BLOOD

When you practice creating art from triggers in the various ways described in this book, you train your body to take bigger, juicier creative risks. Like, "OH MY GOD IS HE GUNNA TAKE THIS THE WRONG WAY??" kind of risks. Once you've taken the time to explore some of the darker, murkier territories within your heart through monologues, scene work, and archetypes, you may feel more confident in bringing them with an element of surprise, like the Goddess of Controversial Surprises that you are.

For myself, meeting my own shadows has been delightfully fun and the aspects of myself that I've uncovered have been a gift when brought into partnership. It shakes things up, brings about something unexpected and stirs up a moment that would otherwise lead to a hamster wheel of collapse or closure.

I especially love to bring the element of surprise when I have nothing left to lose. Here's an example:

The first time Ken and I broke up, it was one month into the partnership.

All of our wounds and triggers were coming up at once, and it simply became too much to hold since we didn't have a foundation of trust yet. After we broke up we spent at least two days going back and forth in little audio notes saying "one last thing!" and getting our final two cents in.

Once the dust settled, I unpacked a few things on my own. I looked at: *where was he right? Where do I stand by my truth? Where could we have met a little more in the middle? What do I want to do about it now? How does creativity want to move through me?*

A little backstory: the first time we ever spent a good chunk of time together, I was on my period. That was exactly one month earlier than the break up, so I was on my moon cycle again.

And I got an idea for how to make some art.

I went to the bathroom and covered my hand in my blood (truly *covered*). And sent him an email, after triple checking it would not go to his assistant, saying "Happy Fucking One Month" with the picture of my blood-covered hand flipping him off.

It was glorious.

A true piece of art.

Worthy of the Guggenheim, quite frankly.

Within the hour, he wrote me back a playful text, something like, "Oh so *that's* how you want to open your heart!" I laughed to myself… and waited.

He then asked, "Can I share with you the ways I could have done better last week?"

I said yes, and he listed out ten things that he would have done differently. He was not only a clear "yes" to receiving my art, but he also followed it up with an immediate apology for our break up.

In my experience, creativity in love creates a natural opening in the heart. It just does. It takes *more* effort to remain closed after receiving a piece of generous art that's come your way.

When two people who are highly triggered and make mistakes as they try to love each other better, *these* relationships often have the most to teach us about where we are not yet healed. Therefore, making art in these relationships (and thereby meeting ourselves in these relationships) has the most potential for profound healing.

By making my period-hand-art, *I was meeting myself.* I didn't send that offering to get anything in particular, I was merely listening to the calling within saying, "Give *it* a voice." But by taking this edgy creative stand, I healed something within. I healed the part of myself who thought she needed to protect herself with unbreakable, rock hard, no-entry walls around my heart. I broke down those imaginary walls, opened and took a risk.

As a result, my nervous system found a new way to embody heartbreak that wasn't just about lying on the floor and crying, but about rising up and rising through. I took initiative in my pain in such a way that it was used as *life force energy*, and not just as can't-get-out-of-the-bed heartbreak or spinning-in-my-head debilitation.

Sometimes anger is going to spiral around in our head. Sometimes heartbreak is going to ask us to mope around for a few days. Sometimes frustration is going to keep us from flirting with the world and living a day to the fullest.

But not always. Sometimes that anger, heartbreak or frustration can be used to *give us energy* rather than take it away. It will generate energy, chi and motivation. It will light a fire under your bum.

It only takes one piece of risky art, like mine above, to reveal that to you. And every day afterwards, you will *know* there are options available when any of these less than stellar emotions arise, should you want to create something with it. The world is now your artistic oyster.

"BUT WHAT IF HE..."

Without fail, at every workshop, somebody asks me, "But what if he doesn't understand it?" or "I've already tried that, and it didn't work."

Your mind is always going to come up with excuses for why you can't create art, or open your heart first. Usually these excuses put the responsibility for the moment on your partner:

- *He* needs to open first.

- *He* needs to be more trustable.

- *He* needs to live less in fear.

- *He* needs to earn my art.

- *He* needs to fully commit to me.

- *He* needs to be more masculine.

The problem with this attitude is that it puts the responsibility in the wrong place. For as long as you are actively choosing to be in a relationship with someone, *you* are responsible for opening through the sticky parts. Not him. You. Why? Because creativity in love takes one initiator — one person who is willing to extend an olive branch of connection. And while your partner may do that from time to time, waiting around for it (and punishing him by withholding your feminine energy when he doesn't) isn't being an artist of love.

This doesn't mean that you bypass your pain — it means that you are devoted to opening *as* that pain. It doesn't mean that you should be the only one putting in effort — it means that you are devoted to putting in *your* effort. Our culture spends way too much time looking at love through a tit-for-tat lens, tallying up the kind of love one person gives versus another. It's exhausting.

My last example is living proof as to why you don't need to wait for anyone to *do* anything in order to create art. Because I took a risk—a pretty big one at that—with a little finger painting and photography, my relationship was given the nourishment it needed to keep moving forward. My vulnerability opened a door to deeper love and connection. Ironically, I didn't even have that as the goal—I just wanted to make something that I knew would feel pretty damn good.

Here are a few common questions I get about being an artist of love in relationship:

1. **What if my partner doesn't understand polarity, and any time I step into the feminine, he does too?** If you find your partner acting like energy more than depth (for example, when you start seductively dancing, he does it with you) you can continue to stay in your energetic lane while also letting him know how much you love when he embodies masculine presence to hold you. You can purr in his ear, "Baby, will you stand strong and tall like an oak tree so I can dance for you?" to give him a little direction, without making it an emasculating command. Gentle guidance with love will go a long way.

2. **Do both people need to be committed to creativity in love for it to "work?"** There are two questions I have for anyone wondering this. Firstly, how do you define "work?" Is there an end result you're looking for other than being fully expressed and serving love? If there's something else you're looking for, be careful. Any kind of expectation you have for how things are supposed to go will, in the long run, hurt your relationship and your artistic heart. Second question is: do you need your partner to also be creatively expressed in order to have a fulfilling relationship? There's no wrong answer to that one—it could be a need for you, or not.

   This could very well be a need for you. For some people, it's more important to *be* fully expressed rather than receive the artistry of another. That said, you could very well have a legitimate need to be in relationship with someone who is also full of creative and artistic expression. Only you can know what is a *need* versus a *preference*.

3. **What if I expose my heart and my partner makes it worse / shames me / dismisses me / hurts me in some way?** There is beautiful potential for growth in a drama-dharma situation where two people's triggers come together…*but*…there is a difference between collapse and cruelty. A collapse can be an unconscious moment where one person simply doesn't have the tools or awareness to deal with the situation, or something is happening that's bringing up a level of fear their body doesn't know how to hold. With time, patience and honest communication, this is something that can be worked on.

   Cruelty, on the other hand, will re-traumatize the heart again and again. The way you can best identify cruelty is if the energy is sharply coming into you from the other person, hurting your sense of self, confidence and vulnerability. You may feel shame afterwards.

   With both instances of collapse and cruelty, you have to decide how long you're willing to remain in devotion to the partnership and work these things through. There's no wrong answer, but I strongly recommend you protect your tender heart at all costs, giving these precious pieces of you to those who see, honor and cherish them. And if you're with an emotional or physical abuser who's *maliciously* manipulative and does not have your best interest at heart, that's *completely* different from what we're talking about. Remove yourself from this situation as safely as possible and with a team of support.

4. **What if my partner thinks it's weird that I'm changing?** Let them think you're weird! Stop spending so much time and energy trying to control others' perceptions of you. It's draining your life force. Make your art and let the chips fall where they may.

Remember your practice as an artist of love with yourself. All art begins and ends with you. Your journey as an artist of love is about unveiling all the layers blocking the infinite ways that love is wanting to move through you. Some of those ways include being weird. Let the awkwardness of being a human penetrate and open your heart into radical liberation and self-expression.

STEPPING ONTO THE STAGE

In this section, you've learned how to become an artist of love in relationship with other. You've learned about the three relationship realms, *imago* partnerships, drama-dharma connections and how to alchemize the core needs and wounds that show up in love.

You've discovered how to use conflict as a pathway to creativity as any four of the main archetypes. You've explored how shadows can be used to create deeper safety in your romantic partnership, and how scene work can support you in expanding your capacity for authentic expression. You've also learned how an emotion like heartbreak can be transformed into a moment of deep generosity!

How incredible is it that the conflict you experience in love gets to now be your pathway into creativity? That every fight is an opportunity to embody art? That each misunderstanding is merely a marker for more of *you* to come online?

With this knowledge in place, you are ready to begin infusing your relationships with creativity, passion, play and devotion. And since every relationship has its triggers, you're equipped to start *using* the crunchy stuff that comes up in life as fuel for your artistry as soon as NOW!

And…

What if you want to go beyond the bedroom, beyond the household and beyond life amongst the pots and pans? What if you want to extend the tendrils of your innovative heart into the households of hundreds, if not thousands of people? What if you want your expression to be not only healing for you, but influential to the hearts of many? Or what if you want to extend your newfound reverence for the feminine into your relationship with earth, herself? To learn how to meet the earth and her natural goodness with the same tenderness you are giving to your relationship?

How you are in a relationship is often how you are in the world. How you crave, reject, mistrust, love and relate to your partner's masculine energy is how you crave, reject, mistrust, love and relate to the masculine of the world. How your partner honors, dominates, protects and relates to your feminine energy is exactly how he honors, dominates, protects and relates to the feminine of the world.

When we enter a relationship, we willingly sign an invisible vow to be our partner's training arena for the great drama of life, and them, ours. When we dive into love, we are given all the opportunities we need in order to transform collapse into creativity, jealousy into generosity, insecurity into ingenuity, and selfishness into the sacredness.

When your nervous system allows itself to learn these profound lessons in love, you then get to receive the incredible gift of living the artistry of love as a lifestyle. Not just inside your home, but also outside amongst humanity.

Your relationship is where you train — the world is where you *transmit*. In the following section, we are going to take the artistry of love one step further, into the world, where you can transmit your essence as an artist of love for all. Let's take a step together onto the biggest stage of all.

Part Four

THE ARTISTRY OF LOVE WITH THE WORLD

THE SPARKLY,
SOVEREIGN THIRD ACT

Becoming an artist of love in the world is the third act for a reason. It is where you, the leading actor in your life, find a renewed sense of your identity and give your story an empowering resolution. Your third act gets to be your sparkly moment of reclamation.

In the first realm, the artistry of love with self, you are focusing mostly on healing your personal vessel and relationship to yourself. In the second realm, you are turning that "me" into "we" and infusing deeper intimacy, truth and artistry into your partnership. Both of these realms are doing the deepest *foundational* work, but they're local to you and the home. This realm, the artistry of love with the world, goes beyond *you*, beyond *your partnership* and into the very heartbeat of society.

The artistry of love with the world is also where you feel the most liberated, because though you're being whomever you want, you also know that your worth doesn't rely on it. You aren't hyper focused on making everything *perfect* anymore. You get to be in communion with everything around you because there is *less* of a focus on *you* and more of a focus on liberation for all. By not taking yourself too seriously, you're everything and nothing all at the same time. The leading actor *and* a mere ornament in god/dess's world. Your art is important, but it's not a meter for your success as a human. The third act is where you play full out because you have nothing to lose.

It's important to note that even though this is the third realm, you've *always* been in it. As a woman, you've been creating art in the world all along, simply because you exist. The hurt you feel, the desire you have, the laughter you share, the anger you radiate — it's all a part of your blueprint.

That said, you most likely have been influencing the world by happenstance, not choice. For example, something in life happens and then you react to it…rather than something in life happens and you respond *powerfully* to it. If you live your life the first way, you're not actively harnessing the power of this third realm. You're doing it by accident, as a *reaction* to your experiences and history of how you have behaved or felt in the past.

When you start to realize that all your thoughts about "who you are" and "what you can do" are an accumulation of those experiences, you can decide to believe something different. You don't have to exist as a *reaction* anymore. You can be a *response*. Life continues to happen, but you summon your strong spine and soft heart to decide how you want to respond to what it's given you.

You can begin to make new choices that lead to better romantic connections. You get to set new boundaries that lead to better protection of your time and energy. You get to reveal yourself in new ways that feel more authentic and juicy. You get to liberate love in the ways *your creative genius* wants to, delightfully surprising the world with your choices.

With the power of third realm meticulous awareness, choice and autonomy, you will be able to *purposefully* impact the world rather than by accident… and you'll be able to do it exactly how you want. You'll learn how to be the change you want to see in the world through the gift of artistry.

EMBRACING THE
MASCULINE OF THE WORLD

The polarity you have been cultivating *inside* your partnership, by turning up the energetic, expressive and creative heat, is a natural reflection of the polarity that will manifest in the world. The deeper you practice energy in your relationships, the deeper you will experience the consciousness of your partner. *Everything* is a manifestation of how you relate with others. And when you find yourself completely, totally, expressive with the entire world, you will know it's because you have been practicing the craft in love.

As you know from the section on self, you have your own feminine and masculine energies within, and you get to develop your own internal polarity through husbanding your feminine. Then, you have polarity with other, meaning you feel *more* feminine in partnership with someone who is *more* masculine — you get to be radiance and energy, and he gets to be consciousness and presence.

Now we have the feminine and masculine dance within the world. As an artist of love, the world is also your polarity partner. If you are here to make a change beyond what happens in your home, you must learn to *feel* the world around you on a more intimate level.

In this chapter, we're going to look at the three different ways the masculine energy shows up in the world: human masculine, nature masculine, and the divine, unadulterated masculine. The human version looks specifically at how the masculine energy shows up in the body of a human. The nature masculine looks specifically at how the masculine energy arrives in nature and the physical world. Lastly, the divine unadulterated masculine looks at purely energy, without any specific form or vessel. All of these versions are important for you to see, understand and know so that you can actively be in relationship with the masculine in all ways available.

HUMAN MASCULINE

The human version of the masculine refers to any masculine energy that arrives in a human. If the masculine is direction, consciousness and depth, the human version of the masculine is *anyone* who arrives in your life to give you direction, consciousness and depth.

Right off the bat, we need to address something important about the human masculine: it doesn't have the best track record when it comes to healthy expression.

For millennia the direction of masculine beings has been mixed. It's been as easy to find poor, unconscious, shallow male energy as strong, capable, and protective male energy—sometimes even more so. Some men have used their masculine power to build, protect, and preserve, while others have used it to destroy, control, and manipulate. This mixed bag of masculine consciousness continues to this day—and while the last decade or so has seen great progress on the positive side, especially thanks to the #metoo movement, there's still a long way to go to universally heal the wounds of all masculine beings.

As we women experience unhealthy masculine energy from the men around us, we are tempted to do one of two things. We may want to reject it completely, envisioning "the masculine" as an old white dude in a suit sneering at us or a gun-toting Marine ordering us around, and refusing to trust any man under any conditions. Or we want to assimilate it into ourselves, seeking to own, control and dominate others in order to feel superior, powerful and safe.

But neither of these responses are actually about "the masculine." They're just about men who have abused their power of have proven untrustworthy. And they completely overlook the other side of the mix: that there are so many men who *do* express masculine energy in a healthy way.

When you become an artist of love with the world, you're responsible for healing your relationship with the masculine *by actively looking at all of the healthy masculine humans out there*. Here are a few examples of how the healthy masculine is showing up for you in the form of a human:

* Your therapist, life coach or reiki guide who holds an impeccably safe space for you so that you can fully let go and relax into the container.

* The reliable, dependable mailman who shows up day after day to bring your mail to your doorstep.

* The Uber driver who gets out of his car to help you with your luggage and then drives you safely and efficiently to your destination.

* A friend that listens and holds space for you when you're having a bad day, careful not to project or interject while you're venting.

* Your father, brother, or cousin who helps you move into your new place, calls you on your birthday, and drops everything to be there when you need them.

* A date who told you exactly where to meet him and at what time, and already had the table ready when you arrived.

The masculine isn't limited to big heroic characters like Captain America. It's also not on the other side of the spectrum, limited to an advertising agency with ten men in boring suits, such as what we see in *Mad Men*. The human masculine is simply that: men who show up with consistency and devotion in the world.

For example, one of my all-time favorite examples of the masculine energy showing up in a human, with all its complexities, is the character Boromir in *Lord of the Rings*. Boromir was crucial member of the fellowship in *The Fellowship of the Ring*. Throughout the film, he had moments of weakness, at one point trying to extract the ring from Frodo, but in the end of the film, he sacrificed his life — by taking several arrows in the chest — to save two other members of the Fellowship. The courage, bravery and complex humanness portrayed in Boromir encompasses a lot of what we see in male culture today. People have easily demonized him because of his faulty moments. That happens a bit with men, yeah? But on the other side of the Boromir coin was deep humility and grief for his lack of consciousness. In the end, his impulse to *save* was much stronger than anything else.

If you want to feel *empowered* in the world, be in an active relationship with the masculine and the men in your life. I encourage you to get to know them better — what do they fear, as a man? What kind of pressure do they experience? What do they want women to know about them? What kind of legacy does he hope to leave?

The point of seeing the goodness of the healthy masculine is not just to see it. It's to feel it deeply — and to trust in *that* goodness of men, so you can heal and transcend some of those potentially very old resentments you may be carrying around. Resentment becomes incredibly burdensome to carry from relationship to relationship.

If you continue to spend time with men who reaffirm the frustrations you have with them, it's time to upgrade your choices my love! Have friends who reaffirm that there are solid, loving, deep men all around (because there are). These are your people.

NATURE MASCULINE

If the feminine is everything that moves and ripples with constantly-flowing life, the masculine is everything that's empty, still and open.

The desert, a mountain and the sky are all forms of the masculine in the body of nature. If we zoom in on a forest, a place I would naturally say is primarily feminine, we will also feel elements of the masculine there. The sturdiness of tree trunks. The early morning silence. The riverbed holding the river.

Whereas the feminine loves energy, moment and change, the masculine wants stillness and nothingness. When you go into places of nature that hold this kind of energetic blueprint you can practice *embodying* that energy within your own life as well as practice *being with it*.

If you struggle to be with the masculine of the world, nature can serve as your practice space. For example, the desert will show you how to be at peace with silence, space and death. He won't talk *at* you, he exists *with* you. All you have to do is blend in and be with him.

If you can't hop over to a desert anytime soon, go outside just before the sun rises, and sit in stillness with your eyes closed. As the sun makes his appearance, let him warm your skin. Invite the heat to become one with you. Listen to the sounds of nature's grand rising.

With eyes closed, imagine you are sitting in the middle of Joshua Tree, Zion, or the Sahara. See yourself with space all around. Zoom out and watch how tiny you become in the great vastness of time and space. Breathe in the quiet. Let the masculine space of nature hold you.

The masculine is the energy that remains calm when life is chaotic; the masculine holds your ground when there is a sandstorm. By embracing the stillness of the desert, you will learn what it means to be in the unknown of the world with grace and ease; you will learn what it means to *hold your ground* with love.

DIVINE, UNADULTERATED MASCULINE

Okay, hold onto your britches my bitches because we're going into the eso-teric. By now, you know that the masculine and the feminine are both ener-gies. They can manifest in people and in nature, but they are always purely invisible energies *first*.

The masculine of the world, without any shape or form to be plugged into, is space. When you go through periods of spaciousness in your life (ex: peri-ods where things feel "too good," you have a lot of down time, everything is running smoothly and according to plan, you're bored) you are experiencing the masculine energetically. This is what allows *you* to be more in the femi-nine. You naturally feel the space and the grounding, so you can fill it with more of your energy, creativity and flow. The polarity is strong, and you are held. Time to let your hair down, run with the mountain lions and dance within infinity.

On the flip side, when you are being met with periods of pure chaos, unpre-dictability and rapidly changing emotions (a breakup, a loss, moving homes, getting any kind of curveball in life), you are being invited to *be* the mascu-line. The feminine is dancing all around you and you need to plant your feet and bear down. While the forest fire is raging all around, you become the penetrating force that obliterates all the bullshit and gets to the core of the matter. Set boundaries, use your calendar, take time to meditate, create struc-ture, take the one next step that will support you. Go mama go.

Everything in life happens in seasons. There will be some ebbs in your life where you need to sharpen your awareness and remain calm in the face of chaos (you lost your job, your boyfriend lost his job, you lost your shit, your boyfriend lost his shit). These are all great reasons why you need to make peace with *the masculine*. It ain't going anywhere. And the more you can be with it, and *become* it, the more you will know exactly how to engage this energy as an ally.

An everyday role that often requires agility between shifting from the masculine to the feminine is motherhood. I've worked with many clients who are mothers and it's always a beautiful journey to watch them harmonize their masculine, which includes guiding, leading and disciplining their child, with their feminine, which includes letting go, being in pleasure, being child-like herself, being in a flow.

Not to mention that motherhood is the ultimate creation of art for the world! You are contributing a new life to a planet who will also influence the world in beautiful, unexpected ways. You are *creating* the gift.

I once had a student named Abby who was a bit of a hyper, anxiety-ridden perfectionist. In the first session of our coaching container, she told me she had just found out she was pregnant. She had originally come to work with me to "be more feminine" and I quickly put together that life had given her the greatest coaching container of all (her nine months of pregnancy) to learn exactly *that* with her pregnancy.

Abby was immediately hit with exhaustion, fatigue and morning sickness, all which kept her from being able to live out the perfectionistic tendencies she usually coped with. She fought her need for more rest at first…but after a few beautiful, open-hearted break-downs (which were certainly a part of her "becoming more feminine" initiation) she softened and learned how to *be with* her exhaustion rather than fight it.

Abby started to rest, relax and create space for nothingness. Instead of forcing herself to perfect her work, she did the best she could until her body said, "No more." This was something she *never* did before. Some days, her body gave her plenty of energy to utilize for preparing the baby's room, ordering supplies, getting the house in order and taking care of her own needs, while other days she was flat wiped. She no longer had the privilege of simply doing whatever she wanted to do, at any given time. The little fetus in her body was already influencing her in ways she couldn't override.

This gave Abby a deep lesson in the art of surrendering, and *trusting* that everything would get done in the exact time it needed to get done. The art of surrendering is a lesson that some women never learn because they veto the body's plea for rest in order to let their get-shit-done mindset take the lead. The "do everything, all the time" attitude is chronic in our society, but a woman's body will never truly placate it. She has her own rhythm, cycles and seasons: ones that overpower the schedules of society. The great miracle and mystery of pregnancy is one of those places.

Through learning how to surrender, Abby learned how to ground and be more present. Ironically, the more she surrendered into her cycles as a woman, the more she was able to deepen her capacity in the masculine—the one in her who didn't *need* to get everything done because it prioritizes depth over "doing everything," and consciousness over "completing it all." She no longer needed to *perfect* something to feel comfortable. She could handle discomfort, remain calm in transitions and be with stillness.

PRACTICE: SEEING THE SACRED MASCULINE

Actively *look* for all the places in the world where you're experiencing the healthy masculine whether it's in the form of another human, nature, or an unexplainable feeling of grounded energy. For example, an appointment that starts on time. A bridge that doesn't break. An online date who is exactly the height he says he is in the app. A book that has a clean, easy-to-read structure. Your father who always pulls through. These are all ways the masculine is showing up for you through relationships, structure, society and energy. You can even keep a Sacred Masculine Gratitude List to keep track of how the masculine is showing up for you already, beautifully.

Here is a list of additional embodiment practices you can pick and choose from to engage *your* masculine energy within:

- **Feel your feet on the earth.** Your feet *are* your sense of grounding.

If you don't feel your feet, you won't feel rooted. As often as you can, ask yourself throughout your day, "Can I feel my feet?" Put your awareness into your soles as you walk to the kitchen, sit at work, teach at your job and take your morning walk.

* **Breathe into the belly.** Anytime you are consciously "holding" something, you are engaging your sense of the masculine. When you breathe deeper, expanding your belly wide, you are practicing *holding* energy. The deeper the inhale, the deeper the practice. Breathe.

* **Meditate.** Sitting in absolute and complete stillness is a wonderful masculine practice. This is your time of no demand: nothing to do, nowhere to go, nothing to be. Just sit and receive. Pay attention to any messages you may receive as you drop deeper and deeper into the quiet stillness—that's where your psychic gold lives.

* **Be present.** The next time you get coffee with a friend or go out to dinner with your family, how present can you be? How intentional can you be with every word you speak and how present can you be with everything you hear? Humans often look for ways to discharge energy when it becomes too much—they leak it out by interrupting others, walking away, exploding or disassociating. Try simply being with whatever is happening and being a *yes* to it. *Yes, yes, yes. I am here for this.*

By doing these practices, you will begin to feel more present and, most importantly, safe. The more you undo the messages, stories, beliefs and resistance you have to the masculine (both in yourself and outside of yourself), the more your emotions will feel safe to exist, exude and create from. You'll have proven to your body that *(1) the world is in fact a safe place and (2) in moments it may not feel safe, you know how to ground yourself into safety.*

When you feel safe in your own body, you can be more present to your own experiences.

When you learn to be okay with moments of discomfort, you will stop relying on unhealthy patterns like perfectionism or avoidance.

When you learn to see the masculine as dependable, you can open up to others more.

Healing your relationship to the masculine is undeniably crucial if you want to feel *all* of yourself available, and open, to life.

EMBRACING THE
FEMININE OF THE WORLD

Mmm the juicy, juicy feminine. She Who is Filled with Pleasure. She Who Radiates Color. She Who Grows Fangs. She Who Dances like Starlight. She Whose Words Cut Like a Dagger or Heal Like a Balm.

The feminine is so much more than the universal, yet half-hearted, descriptors of "pretty" and "sweet." Being raised in the south, indoctrinated by Southern Baptist beliefs, my experience was that women were inherently less than men. No women were allowed to be pastors. No women should be in politics (what if they have a mood swing?). No women should be in sports broadcasting. No women should initiate divorce. No women should have abortions. No women, no women, no women.

These things were coming from the mouths of men in the community, but the women around me were often regurgitating these rules, nodding their heads in agreement. In my observation, it wasn't because their pure, fearless spirit believed these rules were right. It's because they were indoctrinated into these very beliefs from birth — and they were too accustomed, tired or scared to take a stand and demand something different.

Most of these women embraced *femininity* but not the feminine. "Femininity" is a (patriarchal) term that suggests the *behaviors* of a woman (the way she acts, dresses, and behaves) should meet a specific cookie-cutter code. These women were a yes to femininity and the appearance of being women because they were put into that box, and didn't know otherwise.

As an artist of love who is primarily feminine by design, embracing and embodying your own feminine *nature* is the brave path you can embark on to truly rip off all the layers of expectations the world has piled on you. I mean, don't you think it's ridiculously hot and sweaty living inside that triple layered wool coat of "femininity?" Artistry is how you cool off and reclaim whatever the definition of the feminine is for you.

You've already been working on becoming the emotional, intuitive and expressive woman you want to be, from the previous two sections, but now you get to be in intentional communion with the feminine in the world itself. All of the cultivation you've been doing in your heart and your home now gets to blast out into the earth. Let's look into the three layers of the feminine in the world: the human version of the feminine, the nature version of the feminine and the divine, unadulterated version of the feminine. Just like what we did for the masculine, the human version of the feminine will look at how the feminine incarnates as a human, the nature version looks at the feminine incarnating as the form of landscape, and the divine, unadulterated feminine focuses on how the feminine lives purely as energy.

HUMAN FEMININE

The human version of the feminine refers to feminine energy that shows up in the form of a human. Since the feminine is energy, movement and light, *anyone* who embodies energy, movement and unbridled light is in the feminine.

When a child is crying because they caught a fish and can't take it home in their backpack, they are in the feminine. Logic and reason do not matter, they are *purely* living from the heart.

When a woman grieves over the loss of an unborn baby who has tragically passed too soon, she is in the feminine. She is radiating grief from her whole body, surrendering to the oceanic loss that is overtaking her spirit.

The friend you have that talks fast, vibrates with energy, bounces up and down when they feel excited, and expresses their heart through singing their words—yes *them*. They are in the feminine.

The feminine, though, has had to overcome an insane amount of judgment and screwy pretzeling to be seen in this light. And, "the feminine as energy" is still a concept that still goes right over most people's heads. Like the women in my small town in Texas, they still think the feminine is (and can only be) She Who is Sweet and Pretty.

The feminine is also She Who is Not Sweet and Pretty.

She is the white-haired crone who dwells in a cave making healing potions.

She is the feral, wild woman with hair on her legs and hunger on her lips.

She is the passionate mother of three with white knuckles and a burning desire to change the injustice she sees on the television.

A show that demonstrates the unbridled wildness of the many faces of the feminine is *Vikings of Valhalla*. The character Freydis is a deeply complex warrior who has made it her life's mission to seek revenge on the man that defiled, raped and marked her with a cross on her back. She is fearless in her search for this man, and will put her life on the line in order to do what is necessary for her honor. She is a mud-drenched, ferocious warrior with a loving, protective heart. Throughout the series, we witness the intersection of everything that makes up Freydis: raw and romantic passion, blood-thirsty drive, deep grief and spiritual reverence. She is a true fighter *and* a true lover.

The feminine is raw, hungry, alive and fiery. She will devour whatever is necessary if it means liberating the moment to more love. She will die in the name of justice. She will stand up in the face of wrongdoing and set a new path ablaze. She will take the necessary risks with the threat of burning at the stake.

That said, just like the feminine is wild, she is also quaint, sweet and surrendered when she wants to be. She can very much fit into the traditional description of "femininity" with her soft hands and delicate fabrics. She loves to bask in a bath of rose petals and jasmine. She loves all things soft, cuddly and innocent. She just doesn't *only* love those things.

Moral of the story: stop thinking the feminine needs to be any single way. She will *never* fit into a box, no matter how ornate it is. She will *never* mold into the patriarchy's liking, abandoning crucial pieces of herself in the name of society. She will *always* be limitless, ecstatic, constantly-flowing energy.

Here are some examples of how the feminine may show up in your life already:

* A motherly friend who is always there for you when you need a shoulder to cry on, a soft bosom to rest into and a warm cup of tea to drink.

* Your four-year-old niece who tells you the whole truth and nothing but the truth, without worrying about what you might think or if she'll hurt your feelings.

* A girlfriend who fills up your phone with funny gifs, heart-eye emojis and her current dance song.

* A tender-hearted lover who opens up slowly, like a peony unfurling its layers one at a time, leading to the most remarkable intimacy well worth the wait.

* A group of activists in your neighborhood who gather weekly as a community to speak on social justice, equality and inclusivity.

As you read this list, did any one of these in particular make you cringe? Do you feel a slight hint of judgment towards the activist, the energetic girlfriends or the tender, slow-to-open lover? What about if you imagine a bitch, a slut or a girl boss? Notice any kind of feminine flavor that makes your stomach turn—it's most likely not a true reaction, but actually a conditioned one.

You have been made to shame the slut, disdain the bitch or judge the boss babe. This is cultural and manmade. *Goddess* loves all versions and textures of the feminine—none of them being less or more than the other.

FEMININE NATURE

Essentially all of the elements are nature, or, Shakti. There is life force streaming through the crashing current, the orange fire, the jiggling dew and the sway of bamboo. Jungles, forests, oceans, waterfalls, and rivers all transmit that delicious pulse of a feminine land.

The jungle is moist, wild and dripping with eros. The soft, sticky floor of the rainforest beats to the rhythm of a woman's hips. The sounds of the animals create a lullaby of the dark, alluring unknown. The air, thick and heavy, serves as a cloak of creation.

If you want to rewild your heart, go listen to the morning cacophony of waking animals in Hawaii. If you want to learn what it means to grieve, get caught in a rainstorm in Ecuador. If you want to remember how to speak from your heart, listen to singing birds in Peru. If you want to grow out the claws that have been trimmed, revere the land of Africa. If you want to remember what it means to play, explore the terrain of Australia.

And, if you can't do any of that, listen to the sounds of the jungle through headphones as you prowl like a panther through your living room. Arrange a disco ball on your ceiling and play thunder sounds. Sing in the shower.

And remember…at the same time that you receive so much beauty, the (metaphorical or literal) mosquitoes will continue to bite. The snake will go on slithering. The predators will seek their prey. The tsunamis and downpours will get in the way of your scheduled plans.

There is no pleasure without pain. The feminine knows this *intimately* well. As beautifully glorious as it feels to be in ecstatic joy, we must also make peace with our other facets such as being "overly sensitive," "indecisive" or "bitchy." These parts of the feminine are found all over in nature. Do you think a forest fire is concerned with being bitchy? No—all she wants to do is cleanse the land for its literal rebirth from the ashes.

We can learn how to be with our chaotic pieces with love and compassion by seeing how nature does. Just like with the masculine, being in nature is a way we as humans can learn more about being feminine. There is no better role model for the masculine and feminine than nature. They have perfected consciousness and energy. We will always be able to learn more from the waves of an ocean than we can from a self-help seminar.

DIVINE, UNADULTERATED FEMININE

The feminine, just like the masculine, is an invisible force that is always at play. Just because you don't visibly *see* something that looks or acts feminine, doesn't mean the feminine isn't there. It's in *everything*. To say that someone or something has no feminine energy is essentially saying that someone or something is dead. If it's alive, it's got the pulse of the feminine!

The feminine of the world is beauty, chaos, movement and energy. The feminine exists the most in the element of surprise, the great unknown and the natural rhythm of life that beats to her own drum—anywhere there is mystery, she is there.

Society needs structure in order to thrive, but somewhere along the way, we have lost touch with reverence for the *mystery*. In pursuit of creating order, society has dominated and tried to control all that is wild, unpredictable and beyond their scope of understanding. This is the same theme we have been looking at throughout this book: the theme of being put into a box. Throughout the ages, this is what *society* has tried to do with the majestic mystery of the feminine.

One of my clients, Naomi, led women's gatherings in California during the full moon. After about three full moon gatherings, she was concerned that most all of the women who came into her spaces were shy, reserved and a bit shut down. Everyone would wait until someone else opened up in order for *them* to be able to open up. This is a normal side-effect of metaphorical box-morphing. Everyone grows accustomed to shutting down their wildness, weirdness or wetness. It's all too much.

This made Naomi feel awful and a little frustrated! "*Open up!!*" she wanted to tell them. She felt like she was failing as a teacher by not getting any results or big break-throughs that she wanted in these evenings.

In our session, I shared with Naomi that this is exactly *why* the women are in the groups. They can't open up! They don't feel safe to express themselves! And this can't be another space where they're demanded to *be* any kind of way. This can't be another space where they've got to do something in order to make Naomi feel good about herself.

I reminded her that *she* had to be the one to lead them there, and then completely let go to allow the great mystery to unfold. In order to make this space the kind of wild permission slip she wanted it to be, she would need to *become* the permission slip. She couldn't only hold a safe space as the facilitator, she needed to be *in it* with them.

The next full moon gathering they held, she led everyone through an animal practice where together they became wolves, panthers and lions: each animal requiring different kinds of wild movement, sounds and expressions. Naomi howled, and then a few of them howled. She thrashed like a lion, and then a few of them did. She grew bigger, louder and wilder, and then the group *all* followed. Finally, she was taking them out of their habitual reserved nature and into something unbridled, free and probably a little confronting.

As an artist of love, you are a wild permission slip. You *show* people, through your body, breath and movement, how the feminine can truly be expressed. You show what's possible.

The more you can live the wildness, amplify your expression and become your art, the more of a leader and teacher you will be as a byproduct. And no, you don't need to actually become a teacher of the feminine. This is the gift of Woman—you already are, just like you are already an artist in the world. You are, because you exist. The way one woman lives inspires the way another woman lives. We are all mirrors and teachers for each other. When one woman learns to expand and express, we all do.

PRACTICE: AMPLIFYING THE FEMININE

Your medicine lies wherever you shrink in a particular face of the feminine. When you find yourself judging or repressing an expression of the feminine, such as feelings of jealousy, insecurity, neediness, yearning, anger and desire, see if you can *relax open* in the discomfort. You don't have to analyze or break it down—in fact, don't. That gets you into the head and out of the body. Merely *breathe deeper* as you feel your rage or you see someone else in pleasure.

If your body is a byproduct of society, like most of ours, you may feel on a cellular level that the feminine isn't safe to embody (*psttt* *witch hunts, per-secution, stoning, slut shaming*), which is why you'll hold your breath or tighten up when someone else is defying that story. When someone, or some-thing, is unabashed with their feminine, your body may restrict out of fear that whatever is happening is not okay or "not allowed." This takes a shit ton of time and energy—*your* time and energy. Energy that you could be directing elsewhere, like building an epic family, having multiple orgasms and manifesting your dream house.

The good news is this is all learned behavior, and can be completely unlearned by doing the very simple practices in the following….

Relax open to the experience, rather than rigidly tightening around it. Literally unclench the jaw, soften the inner thighs and even imagine breathing in whatever you are witnessing and feeling. Your body, not your mind, is the way to a deeper embodiment—and liberation—of these flavors. By deepening your breath, you deepen your experience of those textures, leading to a new nervous system response that says, "this is, in fact, okay!"

I encourage you to do this when the emotions arise in yourself as well as when you see it in others. The feminine often learns more about the feminine through witnessing others… she learns about her own body, energy, heart and soul through witnessing, observing and even mirroring. By watching how other people embody the feminine, and learning how to "breathe that in," she can teach her own body to let go even more deeply.

Imagine how much time, energy and space you will have to use on creative endeavors when you're no longer directing your gushing river of power towards *resisting* your feminine.

SO MUCH TIME!

Truly, you can get back to writing, making love, laughing, spending time with friends, making money and being the creative muse you were born to be.

Earlier in the book, I talked about how touching an emotion *fully* is the only way to help it dissolve. When you amplify emotions, you can finally touch them FULLY. This is what leads to life moving through the system faster and with more agility. You never *stop* feeling pain altogether, just like you never stop (nor want to stop) feeling pleasure, but it begins to circulate at a quicker rate.

Here is a list of embodiment practices you can do to amplify and expand your sacred feminine, so you can begin to go into life even more deeply:

- **Making sound.** How do you feel? Put it into sound form (even if it sounds weird, ugly or nonsensical). And then make it louder. Sound is how we release stored vibration and can help us vibrate energy through our body. Sound is a form of energy, therefore, it is a crucial part of the feminine herself.

- **Move pleasure (and pain) through the body.** Dim the lights, set out some candles, turn on a playlist that gets you feelin' yummy and lay down on a mat or rug. Begin to move your body in sensual ways (while making sounds) and give yourself the gift of pleasure. Even if it's only a ten-minute practice, you can intimately and somatically connect with your feminine body by giving yourself a container to drop into. If it's pain or grief you are feeling, let it out. Cry on your mat, stomp your feet, and pound your fists. Let it out.

- **Move your hips.** While in the kitchen, while feeding the baby, while brushing your teeth. So much energy is stored in the hips, waiting to be released through movement and pleasure. Make it a practice to sensually indulge in the movement and rhythm of your body by including it while doing regular ol' life.

- **Practice expressing.** We have done a lot of work already on the art of expressing, but to bring it home even more, create a simple practice for yourself where you practice expressing (with as few words as possible) how things make you feel. Even if you are by yourself. Don't like that rotten apple in the fridge? Throw it. Love the new outfit you bought online? Jump up and down and laugh. Don't like that your partner keeps playing video games? Bite the controller out of his hand and walk away like a panther. What emotional performance wants to come through?

By doing these practices, you will more easily become one with the feminine of the world. Think of expression, hip swaying, embodiment and sound-inducing all as methods of communing with the world. You are dancing *with* the oceans. You are swaying *with* women. You are expressing *alongside* Mother Earth.

While the above practices are things I'm offering you to do to get back into your own feminine, these practices are inherently linked to the rest of the world. The deeper you allow, express and embody your own emotions, the deeper you are available for the mystery of the universe. And vice versa! When you allow, and learn from, the mystery in the world, you accept the unknown within yourself.

A SERVANT TO LOVE

When a woman is unabashedly devoted to healing her relationship with both the masculine and the feminine in the world, she's also making it her sacred mission to be the *embodiment* of that sacred union. As an artist of love, she makes it her divine calling to open the spaces she goes to more love by being that love. It's that simple.

And the key to opening spaces to more love is to continuously sacrifice your narrow focus on your personal desires only, and to instead, direct your gaze softly to what love *itself* is asking for.

This is how you move from doing something selfishly to sacredly. It's not *only* about you and what you want—it's about what love herself wants. You are a servant to love.

And as such, you are willing to sacrifice the shit out of your ego if it means being a sacred conduit for deeper, richer love. You'll create art because love is asking you to. You'll dance because she demands it. You'll make peace with your so-called imperfections, because you are nature and nature is perfect. You'll do the things that "normal you" wouldn't do, because you are no longer living just for your own sake.

GIVING WHAT YOU NEVER GOT

No matter how lovely your childhood was, there was something that you needed that you didn't receive, such as physical or emotional safety, permission to be messy, stability, honesty, innocence and/or unconditional love. This is what we have been looking at in each section of being an artist of love, but now it's time to see how this applies to what you offer the world. I believe your destiny, just like your dharma, lives in that act of *becoming* the kind of love you always wanted.

Take a gander at where you close up as an adult. Where do you collapse? Where do you hide? What fears do you have when it seems that others are seeing the real you? In the same way that relationships give you an opportunity to heal those wounds, *life does too*. You don't need to be in partnership in order to turn your drama into dharma. You just need to be in the world.

My client Amelia was single when she came to work with me. She had been practicing the artistry of love on her own, but was craving to take her art further. Together we looked at some of her childhood systems, particularly the ingredients that her household lacked. One of them was frivolous joy.

Amelia grew up with extremely strict parents who cared very little for kitchen dance parties, YMCA father-daughter gatherings or shenanigans of any sort. Her daily routine was school, homework, dinner and bed. She watched the other children be greeted by their parents every day after school with open arms and big hugs, while she had to walk to her dad's car and get inside as efficiently as possible. Very little joy. And definitely no hugging.

She continuously looked for partners who would bring her that playful pizzazz she always felt was lacking from her life, but even when she found someone who offered a morsel of the play she wanted, it wasn't enough. She'd find reasons to reject perfectly good relationships because her nervous system didn't quite know how to integrate the frivolity of joy—yet. It was exhausting to keep getting something she wanted but not know how to keep it.

Amelia realized she needed to teach her body how to become the joy she wanted *first*—and then attract a partner from that sovereign place. The actual satiation she was looking for did not lie in finding the perfect man who could give that to her, but rather in creating it herself.

As an artist of love, it was *her* responsibility to become the walking transmission of that joy. In fact, it was not only her responsibility, it was her divine calling as a woman. *She* knew the pain that came from being starved of joy, and therefore could connect deeply with the nourishment of it—for the world.

The assignment I gave Amelia was to go to the grocery store and sing up and down the aisles like a child. She could skip, twirl, smile at other folks, juggle tomatoes, tap dance holding a peach, blast open a bag of Fruity Pebbles and react like the flying cereal was money falling from the sky—anything she wanted, as long as the action was moved by Joy itself, rather than her mind.

Amelia put her hair in two braids and laughed as she rhythmically danced up and down the fruit and vegetables, picking up pieces and singing about them. At first, most of the people around her tightened up (which is usually what happens) but as she held the pose, they relaxed and softened open, even laughing with her.

Mind you—she didn't know these people's names, and she didn't have established relationships with them either. She wasn't going to do this *only* if these strangers proved they were trustworthy first—she didn't need to. She wanted to practice the art of giving a form of love *without* expecting anything in return.

She opened the entire store. People picking out their oranges with rigid humdrum frowns started laughing and lifting their heads up. Breath flowed into the space. There was a shared experience within the store—a mini moment of community. Amelia felt deeply *alive* and in her most natural element—a transmission of joy.

Being a servant to love will do that. You feel a purpose beyond just your personal experiences. You can feel a bigger reason for being alive and a bigger reason for sacrificing your ego. And that bigger reason, even if it's just publicly singing up and down a grocery aisle, will liberate more of your expression to come into all of life.

THE ARTIST OF
LOVE STAGE NAME

One of my favorite fun tools to use when helping women identify their gift to the world is to assign them an artist of love stage name.

Your stage name encompasses everything you are here to transmit to the world as an artist of love. It should be specific, but also a bit on the esoteric side, and it should really *really* resonate with you. You want to feel your pussy tingle at least a little when you hear it.

A name is like a North Star. It gives you a compass for everything you do. When you feel uncertain or lost at sea, you can look to your name to help you get back on track.

A client of mine, Patricia, was really struggling to move on from all the resentment that had built up due to her loveless childhood home. She was the middle child of seven in a Midwest farming family, and her parents were so focused on the farm that they never truly *saw* her.

Patricia rebelled as soon as she could. Around the age of 15 she started dating "bad boys" who she smoked weed and played hooky with. She was sent to detention on more than one occasion, but her parents never understood or listened to her cries for help. They grounded her, put her in her room and pretended like everything would be better after she learned her lesson.

Patricia eventually retreated into an abyss of her loneliness, attracting partners who fed on that type of blank canvas energy. Since she was taking up very little space, men who wanted *all of the attention* somehow found her. She had grown accustomed to retreating back into her own psyche and tending to the needs of others—and these relationships continuously drained the shit out of her. She was so tired of that dynamic, but didn't know how to break out of it.

Deep down, Patricia knew she had a brilliant secret sauce of love to share with the world and would never be able to do that if she continuously hid her gifts, magic, and energy behind men she dated. She was ready to become an artist of love—inside and outside of partnership.

Together, we first looked at giving her a stage name to serve as her North Star. The way this process begins is by listing out all of the qualities my client wants to embody. For Patricia these included uniqueness, "disco-ball-esque," brightness, light, luxury and color. These were energies she was *not* currently embodying with her totally black, baggy wardrobe and shy, reserved expressions, so it was great to see them on her desire list.

(Note: When creating a stage name, don't limit yourself to only words that feel reasonable or doable. Choose words and phrases that light up your soul, regardless of whether or not they feel feasible. The whole point is to go somewhere new that will lead to deeper realms of liberation, so the more foreign the textures feel, the better!)

Next, we gave Patricia a name that encompassed these qualities—something that would really hit the bullseye of who she wanted to become. For a woman, the artist of love stage name starts with "She Who...."

On a piece of paper we explored options:

She Who Brightens the Night Sky.

She Who Transmits Luxury from her Pussy.

She Who Bursts Magnificence through Love and Light.

After circulating through several options, we came up with the one and only: She Who Squirts Disco Ball Brilliance.

You can really *feel* the transmission of her artistry with this name, can't ya? When I spoke it out loud, her entire body lit up: her face smiled, her spine straightened, her shoulders pulled back. *That's* the sign I was looking for!

Everything in Patricia's life, for the duration of our work together, needed to fit into this one specific criteria: *what would She Who Squirts Disco Ball Brilliance do?*

From how she ate…

To how she dressed…

To whom she dated…

To her hobbies…

To how she walked…

To how she talked…

To how she breathed…

Everything.

She was committed to transmitting She Who Squirts Disco Ball Brilliance everywhere she went, as an artist of love. She was no longer living just to get a particular need met (or survive without it), but rather to *transcend* that need to something even bigger, brighter and more impactful. Her longing showed her how she can best *give* herself to the world—not to be a martyr who never gets her own needs met by others, but to give what she needed to herself first, and from there, offer it to the world.

In an effort to become this epic version of herself, she threw out all of the old, stained take-out menus from local restaurants and filled her refrigerator with juicy, dripping fruit. She donated every single gray and black article of clothing, and filled her closet with bright sundresses, colorful garments and luxurious textures such as silk and velvet. She noticed all of the ways she made her body smaller (by slouching, cowering, lowering her eyes) and spent time consciously retraining her body to rise up, look up and stand tall. She cleared out all of the people from her life who thrived on only taking from her, and made a commitment to herself that she would rather spend time alone if she wasn't spending time with people who *gave* to her as much as they took.

One assignment that I gave Patricia was to set up a small table at a park with a sign that said, "Free Love Poems." The assignment was to write very small love poems for people, without knowing a single thing about them. Patricia *loved* writing, but always felt like her voice wasn't powerful or needed, so she never shared her writings with people.

This one beautiful day at the park, she ended up writing 240 love poems. All of those people went home feeling *unique, loved, and seen.* The very qualities she wanted to embody, she offered to the world.

PRACTICE: CREATE YOUR ARTIST OF LOVE STAGE NAME

* Write down 7-10 descriptive words that describe the qualities you want to have as an artist of love.

* Write down 5 versions of a "She Who…." name that powerfully encompasses this version of yourself. Make it colorful, playful and juicy. Refer to the list below if you need examples of names.

* Narrow the name down to the final one. Circle it and write it on a fresh sheet of paper.

* Look at these main categories of your life: food, clothing, friends, home, exercise, body, lifestyle. How closely are you doing your artist of love name justice when you look at your life? Are you missing the mark? What needs to change to be in devotion to this magical version of you that you are creating? Are these places sparkly, powerful, sporty, etheric, light, vibrant or bodacious enough to really transmit your stage name? Write down 5-10 shifts you are going to make in your life in order to become your "She Who…" name. Be specific.

* As you venture into the world, begin to offer your stage name energetically. Turn her on at your friend's party, at the DMV, at a concert. This may make very subtle shifts from the texture of your presence to the quality of your gaze to the softness of your belly. Feel her essence inside of you and practice living from that place.

EXAMPLES: ARTIST OF LOVE STAGE NAMES

She Who Must be Adorned like a Queen

She Who Glows like a Blossoming Goddess

She Who Cleanses the World with Her Fire

She Who Must be Cherished By All

She Who Lives by the Light of the Moon

She Who Possesses the Hearts of Men

She Who Gushes like a Sacred Geyser

She Who Swells like the Throbbing Sea

She Who Blossoms like Peonies in Spring

She Who Commands from the Power of her Pussy

She Who Radiates like a Million Rubies

She Who Prowls like a Panther in the Night

She Who Must be Fucked like a Queen

She Who Demands the Presence of All

ARCHETYPES IN THE WORLD

By now you know that this book is all about embracing many different modalities and tools for love artistry. While now you have your own artist of love stage name, which is completely unique, bona fide amazing and specific to you, the archetypes also provide their own ways of moving about in the world. Let's take a look at each one.

LOYAL ORACLE

My friend Monica had recently ended a relationship with a man who held quite a few controlling tendencies. Nice guy, but easily motivated by his own insecurities. Because Monica was undeniably loyal, she felt bad if she didn't support him through thick and thin. The problem was, he *always* needed support because he *always* felt he was going through the "thick." This led her to be very depleted and under-nourished in their relationship, and eventually to an emotionally grueling breakup.

Monica shared with me that she usually attracted men who demanded her full attention and obedience because there was a part of her psyche that didn't believe she was worthy of being the one who got the attention, let alone worshiped. She hid behind the needs of others—rather than rightfully claiming her seat on the throne.

She wasn't ready to be in a relationship again for a while — not until she worked on this pattern. She decided that instead of being in service to a *man*, she wanted to be in service to *the world*. She wanted to stop giving away her power and start honoring her purpose in a way that would help her continue harvesting and growing her gifts as an oracle.

She created art through this revelation by creating (and producing) a huge event in her city for women to express their longing for love through poetry, dance and theater. But the kicker was every performer had to meet specific criteria in order to keep the performances at a certain caliber of elegance and high-quality. Nobody was allowed to simply show up and perform unprepared. This was going to be treated like a real, professional show. There was an application process, as well as several rehearsals, and each performer created unique costume designs and elaborate backdrops. This commitment to quality and professionalism fed Monica's desire to be loyal and supportive — not to a partner this time, but to her offering for the world.

Monica's show was a hit. She later created several more beautiful events that held the same high standards. By taking a stand for her art, she healed the part of herself who believed she wasn't worthy of *being* the art worth taking a stand for. She was the show's *director* for crying out loud! She had to walk her talk.

The thing was, after producing such high-quality events, she could no longer date men who took advantage of her good heart. She was on a new trajectory, and to be with a man who was anything less than the *most* supportive would be in opposition to her path.

Monica adopted the artist of love stage name "She Who Must be Adored, Worshipped, and Honored" and created new criteria for every partner who wanted to pursue her, just like she would for casting her next high-class production.

PLAYFUL PRIESTESS

Jessica is an actor who strongly resonates with the Playful Priestess archetype. She spent a lot of time in drama school as a child all the way up until college, learning beautifully gut-wrenching monologues and getting deep AF roles in plays. Once she reached adulthood, she started auditioning for on-camera work such as television and movies, and was a complete natural to the camera.

Jessica loved acting, but she was craving to share something that evoked deeper joy—both within herself and in the world. All of her acting work was heavy and emotional, and she was falling into a martyr's mindset of always having to suffer for her art. Though she loved drama, like the Playful Priestess does, the lack of play and joy balancing that drama had her starting down a slippery slope of anxiety and depression.

Jessica nonchalantly shared something really interesting with me one day. She said that whenever she felt the martyr mindset taking over her waking life, she would dream about dolphins. She'd wake up in the middle of the night, thinking she was swimming in the ocean with her oceanic sisters. It felt like these little messengers were telling her something.

Jessica's artist of love stage name became "She Who Dances with the Medicine of Dolphins." Because that's precisely what dolphins offer—medicine of the heart. A kind of soul delight that heals the aches of the heart. Have you ever seen dolphins swimming and *not* immediately smiled as your heart filled with glee? That's the medicine I mean.

For her artist of love practice, I told her that, no matter how inconvenient it sounded, she needed to take time off acting—as soon as she could manage—to travel somewhere she could literally swim with dolphins. This was not just a trip or vacation, this was a spiritual meditation. A time to unplug, re-center and detox from the intensity and demands of others. This was a spiritual practice that was meant to be pleasurable and delicious (as befits a Playful Priestess), not just meditative or spiritual.

After two months of playing Tetris with her schedule, Jessica organized a trip to Kona, Hawaii. She gave herself *two weeks* all dedicated to meditating on the magic of dolphins. Nothing else.

One morning, she stepped out of her Airbnb and was greeted by the sight of dolphins swimming near the shore. She grabbed her boogie board and ran out into the ocean, hoping she would be able to reach them before they swam away.

Getting closer, she could see the group of dolphins leaping and twirling in the air, babies and mamas alike. She swam out as far as she could and once she was only a stone's throw away, the dolphins swam closer... *to her.* They circled around her, gleefully dancing in the water and welcoming Jessica into their dance. Witnessing this miracle (for the first time in her life) she not only understood, but received a *felt experience,* of what it meant to be liberated, to be feminine, to be fully expressed.

Jessica returned home after her two blissful weeks and within the year, made arrangements to pack up her New York City home and move to the beach of Malibu so she could be closer to nature. Once she got a taste of the water, the sand, and the essence of dolphins outside her doorstep, she didn't want to go back to the grunge and fast-paced essence of the city.

Jessica still loved acting, but she was being called to let go of the city, the hustle and the intensity for a period of time. She wanted to prioritize joy, nature and rest. Though she couldn't afford anything huge from her acting salary, she found the perfect little garage apartment a mile away from the beach and had enough saved up for at least a year.

All of a sudden, she had more space and time to herself. She would spend her mornings journaling by the water and her afternoons being a domestic, joyful bitch. There were beautiful moments of silence and even boredom.

Out of that boredom, she felt her creativity spark again. The emptiness offered space for new ideas to fluctuate into her realm. Jessica began writing short comedic screenplays about the life of an actor in New York City. Then she would condense them into shorter scenes and film them on her iPhone playing all the characters: the casting director, the desperate actor auditioning, the line reader. For shits, she uploaded these videos onto Tik-Tok…and the acting community loved them! She acquired thousands of followers almost overnight.

While TikTok may seem silly for most, for a Playful Priestess *actor* there is nothing quite as liberating as being able to make your own material, exactly how you want, and to be funny as much as you are dramatic.

Jessica's TikTok fame gave her a platform for the work she never got to do as an auditioning actor — while she was excellent at heavy drama, it wasn't the only thing she wanted to be cast into. She also wanted to be light, playful and fun. She wanted more autonomy. She wanted to birth ideas from *her* soul — not just the vision of a director.

Maybe her kind of comedy wasn't recognizable to the casting directors in NYC, but they certainly were by regular folks online. And that felt pretty damn good to Jessica.

EROTIC ENCHANTRESS

My client Amy had sexual trauma in her adolescence, and felt like it was her fault for drawing the attraction of men accidentally. She was told she was a "temptress," and that her being that way was why she'd been traumatized. Her aversion to being a temptress as life went on caused her to create this entire life that left her feeling safe, but in total avoidance her own body, sexuality and feminine heart. She didn't want to be misunderstood in her intentions, so she diverted most of her eye contact with men, walked too fast to get caught in conversation, dressed in ways that could not be "misinterpreted" and set up her entire life to feel safe.

She was in a relationship with an incredibly caring, sweet, passionate man who wanted to give her THE WORLD, but her hesitations with being in her body left them feeling disconnected in sex. She didn't want to reveal her sexuality "too much" because she herself was scared of her own essence.

After a couple years of inner healing work, from traditional talk therapy to the unconventional artist of love practices, she began healing her relationship with her body, sexuality and heart. In our work together, she created art out of her anger by filming little temper tantrum videos, saying all the "FUCK YOU!!!s" to the painful trauma of her past. She wrote haikus about her story and found ways to share it through dance.

She began to open up to her partner bit by bit, letting him into some of the more painful places in her heart so that he could bring love to them. She shared with him about how angry she was for not being protected by her family, and he held her. She shared with him how hurt she was for believing it was all her fault, and he held her. Her vulnerability offered the two of them a pathway to deeper connection and intimacy.

When it came time to assign her an artist of love stage name, I focused on something she could do *with* her body to help get her *into* her body. To me, the speed of which she often walked (head down, eyes-diverted, fast-walking) was doing more to her energetic body than she realized. The fast walking was a part of her body's story around "slowing down isn't safe" and "slowing down gets me into trouble."

She received the stage name, "She Whose Every Move Drips like Honey," and began taking slower steps, no matter if she was walking into her own kitchen or around an office. It didn't need to be sexy, just slow.

Alongside this artist of love stage name, she learned the art of boundaries (the only reason she was walking so fast was because she didn't *trust* herself to set a boundary if her attention was called). She practiced using her sacred no.

"I'm sorry, I can't talk right now but I can chat in ten."

"I'm not available for meeting outside of the workplace, but I really appreciate you asking!"

"I'll see if I can fit this project into my schedule. I'm working on a lot right now. I'll let you know in three days!"

Amy then went into the essence of her home and appearance. She began to fill her diet with local honey and fresh papaya, ordered silk lounge gowns from her favorite boutiques and gradually redecorated her home to look like a goddamn priestess's palace! Golden fabric hung from the ceilings and yummy artwork decorated her previously blank wall. She bought red lipstick and sparkly sheer eyeshadow. It was a bit feminine, naturally, but her partner loved what it was doing for her spirit more than he needed the place to feel gender neutral.

Her space began to make her feel more erotic in her home life. Lovemaking with her beloved felt more fun. She started dancing for him, and felt alive for perhaps the first time in her history of being a sexual being.

After aligning her home life with the sexual essence she wanted to embrace, she looked at the work she was doing in the world. Her career as a marketing consultant wasn't quite hitting the mark as "She Whose Every Move Drips like Honey," so she slowly, ever so slowly (slow like drizzling honey), decided to turn her attention towards *creating* a career that was much more fitting.

She designed her first every course: an online lap dance program for women who have suffered from sexual trauma in their childhood.

Using her handy-dandy marketing knowledge from her former life, Amy built a social media account, created a beautiful marketing campaign, and filmed each video with a professional videographer. This program was a tangible offering that signified the deep, yet delicious, healing that is available when you do the work to reclaim your body, your eroticism and your story.

Her ladies fucking LOVED IT.

Amy wanted to teach *all women* that their stories do not depend on the misbehavior of others and that their essence belongs to them and them alone. Everything—including all the reclaiming necessary to heal—lies in your own body and it just needs some space to be experienced freely. Her program ended up receiving hundreds of women, and it is continuing on as more than just a course—it is a movement.

SACRED DEVOTEE

Another friend of mine, Jillian, moved to New York City and though she was in a city of millions, she felt deeply lonely. Every event she went to, in order to make friends, was centered around alcohol or a level of late-night frivolity that didn't soothe her sacred soul. She didn't want to scream over loud music in order to get to know a date, or a new friend. That said, she tried—and she tried hard.

She went to meetups, festivals, camps and probably hundreds of events searching for a community that felt like home. All by herself, too. Community was her deepest calling, and deepest pain point. She grew up without feeling connected to a larger community, and always peeked "over the fence" at the community her friends seemed to have with their culture, religion and neighborhoods. Little did she know, this pain point would lead to her purpose.

She could feel that her heartache around the absence of community was not specific to her—this was a worldwide issue. Everywhere she went, people were talking about their hunger for deep, real, long-lasting community. She wanted to find a resolution to this, at least for her city, with the hopes that this solution would trend wider and bigger.

As a true Sacred Devotee, she decided to create a ritual—not just one for herself, but one for the world.

Every week, Jillian created a list of conscious events that were happening in NYC. In *meticulous* artist fashion, the list would include all the information one would need in order to decide if they wanted to attend: caveats, need-to-knows, costs of the events, if it was a sober gathering, what to bring, and what time it starts.

This list, which she called *The Joy List*, was available for everyone to join by simply entering their email on her website—all free. Her main mission was to help make the planet a little less lonely, and a little more connected, one event at a time.

The Joy List grew at an exponential rate, and Jillian was quickly being invited onto podcasts, speaking platforms and into corporate spaces. She started to advertise on *The Joy List* and began to create an income from it through community coaching—a niche if I've ever heard one!

Eventually, Jillian published a book called *Un-Lonely Planet: How Healthy Congregation Can Create Change*. Her entire life as an artist in the world stemmed from the thing she desired most.

All of these artists of love women created change *for the world* by following the thread of their desires. And their desires, unsurprisingly, were born through their struggles. Like a flower growing through concrete, tremendous change, beauty and impact can be manifested through the power of a woman's full-bodied yearning.

IMPROVISING

The feminine is moment-to-moment expression. In her purest form, she is completely spontaneous. She is passionate, fiery and quick. She is also slow, melty and dripping. No matter how she arrives, she arrives as emotion *embodied*.

The feminine can't be premeditated. That's not how she works. She is a living, breathing embodiment of whatever the moment brings. She rustles because there is wind. She's ablaze because there is heat. She is sad because she is sensitive. Whatever is occurring, she embodies.

This is why the feminine needs the masculine and the masculine needs the feminine. The masculine brings awareness and context to this moment-to-moment expression. He gives her structure so she can harmonize her feelings *with* action. He ensures she isn't *only* her emotions so that she can function day-to-day and have the discipline needed to do human things. (Remember, I'm referring to the She and He within each of us.)

As an artist of love with the world, the most aligned theatrical practice you could possibly have is *improvisation*. It's unplanned, spontaneous and alive — just like the feminine. Just like the world.

The world has very few plans, at least not the kind we are used to. We can't put "Only Peace, Love and Joy!" on our calendar and avoid tragedy, pain and suffering from then on. We don't know what today brings and we certainly don't know what tomorrow, next week or next year brings.

For an artist of love, this is thrilling. She doesn't know who she is going to become, how she is going to grow, and what art she is going to create. She may be simply writing in her diary today, but will publish a book next year. She may be brainstorming business ideas today, but will be leading a sold-out retreat next summer. She may be in a struggling relationship now, but will be going deep as fuck with her beloved after a year of steady artistry. The future holds great mysteries, and all of them are a big part of the mystery of living.

Improvisation is a kind of theater where the characters, plot and story are all completely unplanned. Sometimes improv will include games that require input from the audience, but no matter what, it's always unscripted and completely improvised.

The *audience* in improv theater is the equivalent to the *world* for the artist of love. Both require spontaneous, unplanned interaction in real time. By using improvisation techniques as a feminine artist, you will learn how to open the moment to more love wherever you go using your sacred instrument of *expression*.

You do not need to join an improv troupe in order to train like an improv artist. I'm going to give you three practices you can do from the comfort of your home to begin re-sensitizing your instincts, freeing your instrument and opening your expressive channel so you can respond, reveal, and revel in your artistry at a moment's notice.

EMBODIED SENTENCE STEMS

The Embodied Sentence Stem is inspired by a practice I learned from the Kimball Studio in New York City. These stems will serve as a bridge between feeling and revealing. Here's how to do it:

- Write down a few sentence stems you'd like to practice with. A few examples of my favorites are:

  » "I've been wanting to tell you…"

  » "It hurt me when…"

  » "Nothing turns me on like…"

  » "I've got a bone to pick with you…"

  » "Honestly? *Fuck you*…"

  » "Come here, big fella…"

- Once you've chosen a sentence stem to start with, stand up in the center of your room. Look at a spot on the wall and let the face of someone you know pop up in your imagination. WHOMEVER you think of first, put their face on that spot on the wall (don't decide to go with someone else—trust the person that arose).

- Begin speaking to them with the sentence stem. For example, your third-grade teacher may have popped up on the wall. If the sentence stem you chose was, "I've been wanting to tell you…" then maybe you'll say, "I've been wanting to tell you that you're my favorite teacher I've ever known. You changed my life. You were one of the first people to ever believe in me and I LOVE you for that. I FUCKING LOVE YOU FOR IT!!!" and so on.

- Keep speaking, allowing whatever needs to come through to come through. If you find yourself getting stuck and losing momentum, repeat the sentence stem again. "I've been wanting to tell you…" and usually, you'll find something new pops up.

- If you notice that you begin to feel heated, angry, sad, or emotional, let that natural emotion come through. In fact, use it! Use the emotion to go even deeper. *What's the thing you've always wanted to say but never have?*

- If you're speaking in monotone, purposefully bring in a shift of volume. *Use the body to get embodied.* For example: speak louder and use your stature to grow bigger. Throw up your arms, punch the air, or stomp your foot. You can also get quieter with your volume. You can hang your head, shrug your shoulders and cock your head to the side in disappointment. The goal is to shift your body, emotion and energy throughout the entire "speech."

PRACTICE: Do one embodied sentence stem per day for two minutes; set a timer so that you can contain your practice and trust the structure's got you. As you deepen in your practice, you can start to make up your own sentence stems and interchange them with emotion. One day you may want to play with turn-on or passion and another day you want to play with regret or disappointment. As you practice Embodied Sentence Stems you'll become more adept at mixing emotions with sentences while also finding *truthful feelings* in it all.

SACRED STREAM OF CONSCIOUSNESS

Stream of consciousness writing is a process where you write every single thought that passes through on a piece of paper. Nothing is filtered, and nothing needs to make sense. Punctuation? Go crazy! Grammar? Doesn't matter! You simply write, sometimes three or more pages worth of material.

While many people have at least heard about stream of consciousness writing, not too many have heard of stream of consciousness *embodying*.

The Sacred Stream of Consciousness is a practice that makes space for your body *and* mind's spontaneity. The following two practices are inspired by the work of world-renowned acting coach Eric Morris, which I first discovered from the NYC-based teacher Sean Folster. Here's how to do it:

* Begin by walking around whatever room you're in. Walk in every direction in a nonlinear fashion. Start to take notice of what you see and feel as you walk aimlessly.

* Begin speaking freely about everything and anything, in no particular order. It may sound something like this, "I want to go on a date tonight. I'm sick and tired of being by myself all day long, cooped up in my apartment. I hate that ugly painting, I should get rid of it! Why hasn't my dad texted me back about my tax question? That's really annoying. I always text him back... probably *too* much. I swear to god I'm not eating soup one more day. I've had so much soup. Probably because I'm cheap! Maybe I'll take myself on a date tonight. Ugh but I DON'T HAVE ANYTHING TO WEAR! Why do I live in Minnesota? I want to move." And so on. The point is to put words to *everything* that pops into your head, unfiltered.

* Eventually, begin to use your body alongside your speech. You may throw your hands in the air, stomp your feet, pout, laugh, jump up and down, play air guitar, stretch, point at things, exclaim with a raised finger, scratch at your skin, belly over, and/or give an "I don't know" signal with raised hands and shrugged shoulders. The possibilities are endless.

* Gradually drop your speech and only use the body. Remember, you're still walking around the room. As your thoughts start to arise, use your body to embody the thoughts and feelings. Keep moving in different and spontaneous ways.

* Bring the practice to a close after 10 minutes.

PRACTICE: This is a great practice to do a couple times per week. Not only will it help you get in touch with your feelings and thoughts, but it will also be cleansing for your vessel. All of these emotions are currently stored inside your body, and the only way to free them is to give them an embodied platform.

As you deepen your practice, similarly to the previous practice, you can play with different emotions. What would it look like if you did this practice like a crazy person? Or if you were whining? Or if you were a 15-year-old angsty teen? What about as a 65-year-old British woman of royal descent? By adding different emotional flavors to the practice, you're bringing different parts of yourself online.

SENSUAL SENSE MEMORY

A very common exercise for actors is a workout for the senses called "sense memory." As I mentioned previously, acting is the experience of finding *yourself* in imaginary circumstances. Sense memory is a process in which you will be able to make those imaginary circumstances even more real—through the memory that lives within your senses. Here's the practice:

* Sitting in a chair, imagine you're doing an activity with your senses. For example…

  » "It's as if I'm drinking a glass of Chardonnay…"

  » "It's as if I'm putting my feet in a hot pedicure foot bath…"

  » "It's as if I'm biting into a Hershey's chocolate bar…"

  » "It's as if I'm petting a puppy…"

  » "It's as if I'm taking a cold shower…"

* Speak out loud the activity you're doing with the words "it's as if…" in front.

- One by one, go through each sensory experience.

  » Begin with the nose: what do you smell? Really, truly, what smells arise from doing this activity? Give yourself about 3 minutes only exploring the sense of smell.

  » Move to sight. What do you see? What does this scene look like? Even if you're not seeing, can you *imagine* what you'd be seeing? Eyes can be open or closed.

  » Move to taste. What tastes arise in your mouth? Move it around in your tongue. Notice the back of your throat, all the way to the pressing of your lips. Indulge in the flavor.

  » Move to touch. What do you feel? Move your hands around to explore the feeling. Notice the textures. Furry? Soft? Hard? Rough? Slimy?

  » Move to sound. What do you hear? What noises are all around you? Does it sound soothing? Disturbing? Calming? Funny? Beautiful? Melancholy?

  » Finally, combine all the senses together at once. Let the orchestra of sensation flood you — and then react to that flood. You may smile, laugh, cry, smirk, get angry. Whatever comes up, let it move through you however it may.

PRACTICE: Do this practice a few times per week. As you deepen in your practice, you can begin to use situations that are specific to love, feminine expression and whatever it is you're longing for in life. Maybe your beloved is rubbing your feet, or you're being made love to, or you're being blasted open by a penetrating waterfall. Create whatever scenarios you want to play with, and watch how your body will gradually become *re-sensitized* to sensation.

In a world that has told you to "stop being so sensitive," I'm telling you to *start* being so sensitive. Welcome in sensation, spontaneity, improvisation, responsiveness and impulse. These aspects are the deepest artform your feminine when partnered with awareness and love.

By doing any of these three practices from the comfort of your own bedroom, you'll begin to retrain your feminine body and heart to be responsive as an artist in this world. You will have greater sovereignty and agency over your artistic expression and how you choose to reveal it.

Additionally, you'll feel more alive. You'll no longer be wondering, "How do I feel about this? Am I overreacting? Am I indeed hurt by this? What do I want? What do I need? Is it silly to need this?" Instead, you'll *know* what you feel. You'll *honor* what you need. You'll be able to *reveal* your heart through your body rather than only being able to speak long winded answers about what you think you're feeling.

Ironically, theater will re-teach you how to be real. It's society that's taught you how to avoid the truth. Women are built to be in the moment, here and now. Others may have tried to mold you into being a responsible, self-sufficient, totally non-crazy, non-sensitive, rational creature of measured proportions, but that's just never going to cut it. And it's also not in the best interest of passion. Let's bring back your quick-witted, sensitive self. Let's throw to the wayside rationality for a moment and play with what life is bringing you *now*.

Your improvisation practices will deepen your skills as an artist of love because life happens in real time. Womanhood becomes a whole lot easier when you give yourself permission to simply be human, make human faces and have human experiences. It doesn't need to be *so* complicated—but it does require devotion to the practice of re-sensitizing. For so long as you are an artist of love, you are an artist of the body.

PILLARS OF PROTECTION

Whether or not you are actively going out into the world to transmit different flavors of your feminine, you are. Simply by being alive and living amongst other humans, you are being an artist of love with the world. And while that's a beautiful and powerful thing, it can also be a frightening one.

When you make art for and with yourself, it's easy to feel safe. After all, no one ever needs to see or know about it except you.

When you make art for a partner, there's often more anxiety and nervousness. What if your partner doesn't get it or isn't open to it or thinks it's weird? But in most partnered situations, being ready to make art for your partner means you feel at least somewhat safe and supported.

When you make art for the world, you are subjecting yourself both to the criticism and approval of random strangers, colleges, lovers and friends. (For the sake of this chapter, we will continue to give the word "art" a broad definition, referring to both emotional art, like the embodiment of the archetypes, or an actual creation such as poetry, design, pottery, rap or a video.) That can be straight-up scary!

If your nervous system is highly sensitive to the projections of others, you will need to learn to protect yourself by turning criticism, if/when it comes your way, into creativity. Otherwise, if the criticism of the world doesn't have an outlet, it can lead to a self-shaming spiral.

Yes, criticism can really sting, and rejection can really hurt. Even advanced, experienced artists of love deal with that pain. (I certainly do!)

Here are four Pillars of Protection you can use to create additional safety for your vulnerable heart as you venture into the world to express, transmit and be seen as an artist of love.

1. Get goddamn good at boundaries. You will notice that as you create more art, you will begin to radiate a very special kind of aliveness that people intuitively want a piece of. You will be invited out to coffee by strangers. You will be hit on. You will be invited to hang out with someone so they can "pick your brain." You will receive random DMs in your social media, fan mail, pigeons with little love notes attached to the ankles. And you will be expected to welcome all of these things and give all of these people what they want.

Be careful who you let into your energetic realm. If you start putting these people's requests above your own needs, you will burn out faster than a firework. So don't do it. Not every DM needs to be opened. No, you will not have your brain "picked." You've got plenty of coffee at home. The pigeons can fly to some other person's roof.

If you're a woman, you have most likely been *conditioned* to think it's mean to say no. But you know what's actually mean? Betraying your feminine spirit!

You have writing to do! Creating to do! Feelings to feel! Practice to practice! I'm not insinuating you should become a monk, but you *do* need to learn how to prioritize space for both *feeling* and *creating*. Be picky who gets the biggest chunk of your time. It is not mean to have boundaries. It is a deep, deep act of self-care.

And even with the people you *are* close to, be aware of how often you spend time with them. I have six very close friends whom I love dearly. But I spread my time out with them in such a way that I can continue to deepen my friendship with them *without* losing myself in the relationships. When I go through periods of writing, I normally have to write a text to each of them to set up expectations, such as, "Hey love. I am so excited to spend some time together soon. I am going to completely prioritize writing my book for the next month, so I won't be able to tend to my text messages as much, and I won't be able to hang out as frequently. How about we get a time on the calendar for next Tuesday from 3-7? Things will be calmer after my deadline on XX date." This way, I can remain in control of my schedule at the same time that I can tend to the friendship.

2. Create your art for you. Okay, I know this concept seems a little counter to the idea of making art *for the world.* But here's the thing… you're making art for the world *because* it's for you. If you simply go into making something, anything, *to* open the world, it now has a job to do. It needs to do something in order to make it "worth your time and energy." Yikes.

But…if you make something for yourself because it lights you up, heals you, opens you, refreshes you, or sets you free…*then* the world reaps the benefits. The world gets to receive your ooey-gooey, opened, lit up, joyful, refreshed, fully expressed self because you are doing whatever it is *you* need to do in order to clear your vessel. The world *loves* that shit.

Make the movie because it's a story you need to tell. And then play full out with it. Take a mini short film class. Invest your money. Hold auditions. Organize table readings. Book the perfect location. Create an official call sheet. Get donuts and dip for the crew. Take as many takes as you need to get the perfect scene. Hire a post-production crew. Color-correct and perfect the mood. Send it to film festivals. Get on a podcast. Be devoted to the process from start to end.

Make art because it's how you heal. Your best art will in fact come from your truth. Your womb, heart and intuition know *exactly* what needs to be expressed…and taking yourself away from that knowing will lead to a piece of art that feels stale and boxy. Your art needs *your* experience in order to open the world. And *your* weird, crazy ideas.

The more you find yourself thinking, "Huh…I wonder if *this* could possibly work!" the more on track you are.

Yes, whatever you make will be for the world. But start within yourself.

3. Have discernment. Sometimes art will be an emotional expression and other times it will be an actual creation. For example, maybe you want to spend a full day exploring your inner sacred slut and you want to transmit "sacred slut" everywhere you go. Learning how to dress, eat, act and live like an archetype is a *very* special practice because, like monologues, it will implant a part of your psyche into your body on a deeper level. I love that for you.

But some energies like the sacred slut, dominatrix, and innocent maiden need a protective field in order to be done safely. You don't want to fully embody the sacred slut in a dark alley or the innocent maiden in a board meeting. If you do, not only will you be met with the repressive opinions of the patriarchal world, but you may actually put yourself in harmful situations. We want to make sure you are protected emotionally, energetically, physically and spiritually as you do embodied character practices.

A wonderful practice to do from the comfort of your own home is to practice "turning on" different archetypes on a scale from one to ten. *One* should be hardly noticeable on the outside, but on the inside you may feel a subtle heightening of an emotion or texture. Perhaps you allow your heart to open just a little more, or your sexuality to radiate through your womb just a touch.

You'll then move up to *two*. This will be slightly more noticeable. Maybe your eyes shift, or your fingertips gently sway. Continue going up the scale all the way to *ten*, which by that level, should be *outrageously* amplified, to the point of being nearly grotesque. At a ten, you're slobbering with desire, orgasming with pleasure, howling for attention, humping a chair leg.

The goal is to learn the entire spectrum so that if you're in a public place, you can land on a two or three easily. This way, you can still feel the part of you that is in pleasure, or in her queendom, but it's not on display for others. And then you can turn it up to a five, six or seven when it feels safe or right to do so.

4. Trust the artist of love cycle. If you make a piece of art, give it to the world in some way, and end up feeling unseen, unheard or misunderstood—*use that to go back in!!* The artistry of love is meant to be self-generating, meaning it will find a way to keep going through itself. You'll make something for yourself to tend to your heart, you'll bring that fuel into your partnership, you'll blast it out into the world and then you'll probably be hit by something unexpected that will then be tended to in the privacy of your home. And so on. You are a water-wheel of creativity—a never-ending infinity sign of expression. You *never* have to fear running out of ideas.

The beautiful thing about the three layers of artistry is that they feed into each other. See the world's simplest diagram below.

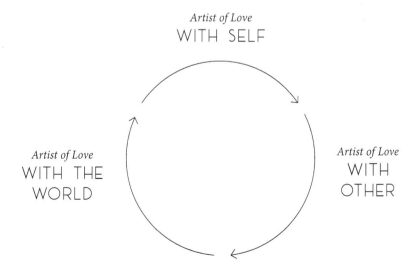

Artist of Love
WITH SELF

Artist of Love
WITH THE
WORLD

Artist of Love
WITH
OTHER

Every time you create something for the world, you will usually be gifted the opportunity to feel a new texture within. Maybe you feel raw and exposed. Maybe you feel imposter syndrome. Maybe you feel something from your childhood pop its ugly head out, saying you're unlovable. Maybe you feel self-conscious, or like your expression was too much.

All of these reasons are a great excuse to go right back into the cycle, starting with the artistry of love with yourself. How can you hold yourself back to equilibrium? What can you create for yourself, depending on your archetype and stage name, that will take you deeper into the heart of your power and creative spirit?

This cycle is self-generating, just like the ancient Egyptian symbol the Ouroboros: a serpent eating its own tail. You are being reborn into yourself: each piece of art you create is a process of devouring what *was* in order to create something *new*.

Oh, and by the way, when you do receive criticism or rejection from the world? Now you can turn that shit into even more art. If someone says, "Hey, *you*! Your art SUCKS," you will have a whole colorful array of paintbrushes to respond with. You can throw an online or in-person *My Art Sucks Party* for all the artists out there bravely taking creative leaps. You can write a screenplay about it, personifying the criticizer in hilarious, yet ironic, ways. You can rent out a Rage Room where you can break shit and scream at all the online trolls of the world (as you pound a TV to smithereens). You can create a Spotify playlist for the lowly artist that needs to remember *art is why we're here*. Whatever happens to you *in* the world, you can respond with artistry *for* the world.

Part Five

CONCLUSION

COMMITTING
TO THE THEATER

Everything in this life is creation. A moment, a feeling, a thought, a relationship, a flower, an adventure, a conversation, a birth, a death, a movie, a drawing, a song, an emotion, a synchronicity, a friendship — your entire life is a theater, and you are the leading actor.

Are you going to play full out? Are you going to create incredible backdrops? Are you going to infuse ceremony into the mundane? Are you going to let go of the other actors who aren't showing up to rehearsal? Are you going to hire the best orchestra with the most exquisite music? Are you going to adorn yourself with the finest of fabrics and costumes? Are you going to write scenes that both break hearts and remind the audience how to truly love? Are you going to use your emotions to alchemize dharma? Are you going to take the time to do the work? Are you going to silence your cell phone and pay attention? Are you going to open your heart as you open the curtain?

If you imagine that all of life is a theater — your theater — you can begin to commit to the colorful, sacred drama it's asking of you. Life is asking for your expression, creativity, and energy — no doubt. But in order to do so, you're going to have to willingly walk into the fire, fall on your face, break a leg and take the damn risks. Art is inherently risky. It's meant to be.

When you originally picked up this book, you were looking for a way *out* of the box the world was putting you into. Perhaps you felt like an animal backed into a corner, looking for a way to claw your way free to the other side. Maybe you felt like a caged bird, losing her will to sing after being overlooked so many times. Or maybe you resonated with the phoenix, but with no idea how to rise from your flames.

Creativity is how you heal, claim and rise from the flames, over and over again. It's a never-ending cycle of rebirth — *you* are a never-ending cycle of rebirth.

Every time you fall in and out of love, you are being presented an artistic opportunity on a golden platter. You are invited into deeper expression, wider creativity and more radiant expression. You are invited into the abyss of your longing to create a lavish new language, which is your heart's message.

When you decide that you are the alchemist of your own existence, you can turn all water into wine. Your life is full of endless possibilities of who you get to be, what you get to receive, and the life you get to live.

MELISSA

As we near our completion of this journey together, I would like to leave you with an example of what's truly possible on this path as an artist of love.

A student of mine, Melissa, originally came to me hoping that if she learned how to be more womanly, she would meet her beloved. Like most women, she had a lot of ideas of who she needed to be in order to be "worthy" of the man she wanted — she needed to be *more* feminine, *more* sexual, *more* open, *more* beautiful.

While feeling more feminine, sexual, open and beautiful are all delicious byproducts of the path of an artist of love, they are not the best goals to begin the journey with because by inherently wanting to be feminine, she was putting herself in the category of *unfeminine.* By wanting to be more sexual, she was automatically disempowering the sexuality she already had. She was labeling herself as someone who wasn't enough of all of these things already and needed to be *more* in order to be worthy of love. The not-enough-game is another way we find ourselves in a box.

To begin, I supported her in claiming the fact that she is already a feminine, sexual, open and beautiful being! And instead of wanting to be *more*, to focus on being *with* what was already there. Instead of falling into the comparison game, or another trap of society, be *with* the magnificent canvas already available. Instead of looking at all the other women, comparing their feminine to herself, to honor that everything she sees in them is also in her.

Early on, I discovered that Melissa spent her entire life moving homes every two years in a military family. Melissa would have to say goodbye to her friends with every move, and there was no room for being emotional about it. She would often be reminded that friends are only ever temporary, and not people to get attached to. When she got her period, her mom didn't have any wise words to share. When her big brothers "playfully" picked on her and she cried, they told her to toughen up and stop being so sensitive. When the family got into a fight, the argument would get swept underneath the rug and never discussed healthily. "Just move on" was practically the family motto!

As a young adult, Melissa often sped through both her work and personal projects sloppily. The furniture in her house was thrown together without a heart-centered vision, the food she ate was simply whatever was around, the clothes she wore had no connection to her identity, and the partners she chose were generally whomever gave her love, rather than being her true match. Deep inside, she was still thinking, "Why care about any of that stuff if I'm just going to *move on* soon anyways?" She didn't go *deep* into anything, because why bother?

Melissa was living what life gave her, rather than what she wanted to give life. This was really where her desire to become "more" came from. It wasn't even really about being more of something, but more about being present to who she is, what she feels and what makes her special. For the first time she wanted to be fully, completely, unabashedly, courageously *herself*.

Knowing that she struggled with the deeper meanings of life and lacked an intimate connection with the Divine, I decided to support Melissa in embodying the Sacred Devotee archetype. Because the Sacred Devotee is connected to god/dess in all things, she would inherently learn how to become one with the goddess in herself by partaking in ritual, prayer and ceremony. She would *feel* that connection with something bigger than herself.

Melissa resisted this idea at first. When I talked about "seeing the Divine in all things" and "letting your emotions penetrate your heart," she stared at me like a deer in headlights. I asked her to trust me, even if it didn't completely make sense yet, and she said yes.

In the first phase, we looked at how she could create art out of her childhood upbringing so that she could begin to unravel the great big ball of tangled yarn that was her conditioned, dense psyche. I knew that in order to see life as sacred, she needed to resensitize, welcome her emotions and feel her feelings a little more deeply.

She began by creating small rituals inside of her private home life: rubbing rose oil on her skin before bed, buying fresh flowers at the market each week, and getting a few small ceremonial tools for herself, including tarot cards and crystals.

Since Melissa was single and didn't have a partner to do ceremonies with, she began to create small rituals in devotion to her *future* partner. She bought a nightstand for the other side of the bed (instead of just having the one on her side) to tell the Universe her bed was ready for him. She hired a few private sessions with a chef to learn some meals she would be able to impress him with. She created an artist of love altar, which was specifically in devotion to

the kind of love she desired to create. On it were rose quartz crystals, images of movie couples she loved, a few small candles, an anointing oil, and a chalice to represent the "holding" of the dream. She found ways to *be in partnership* as a Sacred Devotee without even being in partnership. She felt "him" before he even arrived.

Melissa began to write a love poem and prayer to the Divine every day—for forty days. At the end of the forty days, she went through one poem per day, sitting with the emotions it brought up and tweaking the words to get them just right. She found the perfect female editor who she trusted could support her in channeling the deepest transmission available (she, like a true Sacred Devotee, practiced *meticulous selection* rather than choosing whichever person was the cheapest or first to arrive). They worked together on these forty poems and overtime she created a poetry book she wanted to release into the world. She was entering the third realm as an artist of love.

But…there was one more piece she needed to complete: the book cover. She asked her heart, "What is the cover the Divine is asking for? Which cover will liberate the most love for all?" As she considered this, she reconnected with a creative director friend…who not only helped her develop the most beautiful colors for her book cover, but later also became her romantic partner.

He was smitten by her poetry, her heart and the woman he saw before him. They are still together today.

Melissa's book of love poems to the Beloved led her to her actual beloved. The Divine works in miraculous, mysterious, beautiful ways when we allow our inner artist to dance with the great love language of longing.

[handwritten notes]

- devote to future
early morning
have + made up
learning lines
water to dead like
- what

feel it before it arrives.
how?
would that you do?
need?
live?
alter.

ALCHEMIZING FOR ALL

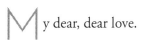y dear, dear love.

Do you know the kind of sex a woman has who is fully embodied, creatively expressed, relentlessly open and in cahoots with her deepest knowing?

Do you know the kind of intimacy that is available when a woman stops internalizing all of the false messaging others put on her, and instead, trusts the inherent wisdom streaming through her veins?

Do you know the kind of penetrating beauty a woman can receive when she prioritizes pleasure over productivity?

Do you know the kind of love that transmits out of a woman whenever she makes it her sacred spiritual duty to embody the kind of love the world needs?

Let me tell you—fucking amazing sex, obliterating intimacy, gloriously penetrative beauty and deeply nourishing love.

This woman is living life on her own terms, setting each box society tries to put her in ablaze, and uses art as a way to metabolize any dogmatic shit that isn't hers to carry.

She is living in harmony with the masculine energy of the world, and she is in cahoots with the feminine of earth. She knows how to become both the riverbed and the river, holding her gushing flow with a bed that won't break.

From her mind to her womb, she is channeling everything she thinks, feels, intuits and knows through her heart. She gives herself space to fall apart when needed, even if it looks like crying on the bathroom floor for hours. And she equally summons the mojo required when it's time to stand on her own two feet and do whatever hard thing needs to be done. She is a fully feeling woman who *knows* what to do to clear her creative channel so that she remains sovereign.

In a relationship, she creates art out of conflict, holds her own emotions and makes space for her partner's. They are in a dance between structure and flow: sometimes they communicate with words, other times with only energy. Sometimes she blesses him with a taste of her eroticism, other times she surprises him with her tender heart. They continue to deepen their commitment through ceremony and gifts, re-choosing each other every day, over and over. While there is certainly conflict, she has a new way to work with it that's not only expansive and inherently growth-inducing for the relationship but also a yogic practice for her creativity.

And then… she goes into the world. She creates something for *everyone* to see. After all the healing, feeling and revealing done behind the door, she dusts off the pearl of her highest truth and makes something out of it the entire world may witness. She is a fully, creatively expressed woman—she is art herself.

And so, she steps onto the grand stage to make her appearance. The curtain is drawn. She is ready to be fully seen in her full expression. And while this also means she is more available for the criticism of others, those judgments become *more* of her creative fuel. She is a mushroom in the forest, eating everything that decomposes and returns it back into the earth. She is a recycler of repression. She takes the tiny nuggets that have been overlooked, dismissed or shut down because they were too big, too frustrating, too unjust—and she gives them a voice. She makes them *good*.

This woman, my love, is you.

And now you're ready to become her.

YOUR FINAL
SACRED ASSIGNMENT

Throughout this book, you have learned how to embody all four of the Artist of Love archetypes in great detail. You are familiar with their golden key, Achilles Heel, artistic flavor, creative strategies, and exemplary goddess/character archetype.

At any point, you can invoke one of these goddesses in your life, relationship and in the world. Just like the old "What Would Jesus Do (WWJD)" you can pull a WWSDD? Or a WWEED?! Or a WWLOD!! Or of course a WWPPD! Take your pick from any of these strange acronyms and create from the seat of your power.

If you'd like to discover which archetype is your *primary* archetype, you can do so by taking the quiz on my website: http://maddymoon.com/quiz

I specifically chose not to mention this until the very, very end because I don't want you thinking this is your only archetype. You are all four—and more! But you may also have felt drawn to one in particular as you read…so this quiz will help you connect with the archetype you'll likely embody the most closely and often.

While these deliciously feminine archetypes will be a compass for your artistic soul, there are thousands more to choose from when you want to expand even wider—and all completely imagined by you!

For example, your stage name as an artist is ever evolving depending on what transmission you want to send into the world. One month you may want to be She Whose Lips Magnetize the Most Conscious of Kings and the next you may shapeshift into She Whose Fangs Slice through Radical Injustice.

Choose your transmission wisely and create a conscious playdate with yourself through it:

As you go to your closet, what outfit would *that* stage name wear?

As you prepare breakfast, what meal would *that* stage name eat?

As you sit down for work, what music does *that* stage name listen to?

As you text your partner, what gifs, emojis and punctuation does *that* stage name use?

As you speak with your friends, what facial expressions does *that* stage name make?

As you gaze into your beloved's eyes, what emotion does *that* stage name reveal?

In order to keep refining and evolving your transmission, I leave you with one final assignment.

I invite you to create a new stage name or choose a different archetype *every full moon*. After reflecting on everything you created, and all that you became in the previous month, ask yourself, "Who do I want to become now?"

Full moons offer a monthly opportunity for starting again. For fresh beginnings. For new chapters. For theatrical intermissions. Within one entire moon cycle you can have three acts as an artist with the same stage name. You can do deep work as a woman, as a lover and as a being in the world, blasting your essence for all to see.

What if, for every moon cycle, you commit to truly, deeply living as your transmission? You move *as* your emotion. You dress *as* your heartbreak. You eat *as* your jealousy. You laugh *as* your longing. You walk *as* your love.

How would your life change? How would you date? How would you speak? How would you breathe? How would you feel pleasure and consciousness? How would you dance between yin and yang?

I truly and sincerely hope this book has given you new, fresh and exciting tools to bring into not only your relationships, but also into your very being. For you. When you take these practices and embody them so that you may walk as a transmission of love, it will inherently infuse into your relationships and love life. In fact, when you commit to the theater of love, your entire life will change.

CLOSING THE CURTAIN

When times feel inherently challenging, or love feels far away, remember that you are and always will be a beacon of love, a bounty of expression and a radiant beam of light. When you ground yourself into this truth, you can open wider as the love you already are. You can strip away anything that is in resistance to your inner ocean of devotion.

As an artist of love, you now know how to: bust out of societal boxes, create art out of your triggers, use monologues as a spiritual practice, transmute your life's drama into dharma, embody both the feminine and the masculine (with self, other and the world), reveal your longing to a lover, learn how to be more of *yourself* through watching TV and film characters, make ceremony amongst the mundane, open the moment to more love through your eroticism, bravely infuse play into a moment of tension, offer gifts from your soul, live as your artist of love stage name, deepen your relationship with your creative spirit, fall on your face and risk it all in the name of love, and finally, become a full-spectrum woman with a full spectrum of feels.

Life is going to keep giving you opportunity after opportunity to find yourself back in a box, but now, you're going to be able to call it and spot it. You're going to see it and say, "Hey, that doesn't look nearly as comfortable as the unlimited, sparkly chaise lounge of mysterious creativity I have created for myself back in my creamy dreamy palace of self-love and liberation. I think

I'll go there, rather than back into an oppressive hellhole, please and thank *yewwww*."

The Artistry of Love is a lifestyle — forever. It is not something you read once and then understand completely. Every day offers you a new opportunity to meet your inner artist, whether it's in connection with only yourself, your beloved or the world. It's an endless cycle, just like the dark, mysterious abyss of your womb. Out of the darkness comes light — your light. The light that is going to change the world.

As an artist of love, you have unlimited tools at your fingertips. I have shown you how you can become an artist in a thousand different ways, through acting, drama, comedy, playfulness, skits, gifs, videos, nature and your sexy, sexy sex. You are built with all of the tools you need inside of your one body, but you can also use any modality that is available to you: paint, pottery, digital art, music, poetry, arts and craft, videography, photography, interior design and creative writing.

The world is your creative oyster and the pearl is your pain. If you're feeling stumped on where you begin creating, simply look at what is currently happening in your life — right this instant. What do you feel *meh* or *ick* about? We usually don't have to search too far.

Create from *there*. Transmute that meh into something gushing with marvel. Only you can witness it or you can extend it out into the world. It is your choice.

This book is my offering to the world. I have been practicing the artistry of love alone, with a partner and now — with you. Every moment of creating this book, I have been committing to the theater. I devoted myself to playing full out with every line, sentence and detail because the art herself deserves it. I sincerely hope you find that this book has changed something deep within your primal core as a limitless woman. You are powerful, exquisite and undeniably mystical. You are because you are Woman. You are inherently a creator.

As long as you remember that you have the infinite, nonlinear, wild world of artistry living inside the jeweled caves of your heart — you will never forget who you are.

WHAT'S NEXT, M'LADY?

If you're wrapping up this book, and saying, "Wow that was AWESOME, and I am completely satisfied and indefinitely complete!" then YAY! You got what you came for.

If you're finishing and saying, "Wow this was AWESOME, but there's so much more and I'm a glutton for depth and devotion," then you can journey deeper with me!

In the resource section to follow, I will share with you the options for further exploration as an artist of love. The deepest work will always be done—no matter what avenue of studying—when the physical body is involved. The cerebral land is beautiful, but the somatic land is where the body *changes*. When you use your voice, and you are held accountable for doing the work, you can guarantee generational healing.

I applaud you for completing this book in full and I thank you for your devotion to the work. I have *always* wanted to write a book on this topic since nothing like this exists, and putting this baby out into the world is a part of my own artistry of love journey with the world.

If you enjoyed this book, I'd deeply appreciate a review from you on Amazon or Goodreads. Thank you for your heart, art and spirit. Sending you oceans, rivers and waterfalls of love on your journey in devotion to love above all.

RESOURCES

PROGRAMS

Creativity in Love: My deepest and most intimate offering; an advanced practice group. With only a handful of women accepted per year, this group container is where everything you've read in this book will be practiced in real time. Shadow work, polarity, performance, sacred theater, artistic triggery, the three realms, embodiment practices, breathwork, stage names and more, this program is for the woman who is ready to go deep. If you want to find yourself in an intimate container where you're devoted to becoming a true artist of love, you can apply here: http://maddymoon.com/creativity-in-love

1-1 Private Mentorship: If you are ready to dive head first into the magical world of feminine embodiment, artistry, polarity and relationship, and you desire to receive a private mentorship as you do so, apply for my private six-month coaching program on my website, or going directly here: http://maddymoon.com/coaching

FREE

Artist of Love Archetype Quiz: While you are designed to embody all four archetypes. I have created a quiz for you to discover which archetype you most strongly resonate with. If you would like to take the Artist of Love Archetype Quiz online, you can do so here: http://maddymoon.com/quiz

Podcast: Listen to eight years' worth of conversations and lessons on relationships, building a business, astrology, spirituality, acting, breakups, family dynamics, anxiety, becoming your own permission slip, body image, eating disorder recovery, movement, play and so much more. Subscribe to Mind Body Musings on iTunes, Spotify and everywhere else podcasts can be found.

SOCIAL MEDIA & WEBSITE

Instagram: http://instagram.com/madelynmoon

Maddy Moon Website: http://maddymoon.com

ACKNOWLEDGMENTS

Dad—Thank you for supporting this book and the words that needed to be shared in it. I love your spontaneous three o'clock phone calls just to see how I'm doing. Please don't ever stop.

Hannah—Thank you for being my big *seester*. I love the woman you are, and the care you continuously bring into your community.

James Ranson—You're the personal trainer of editors. Thank you for always encouraging me to dig a little deeper and go the extra mile to write what's *really* wanting to come through. I am so grateful to have found you.

Torie Feldman—You are such an amazing friend. Thank you for celebrating me every step of the way creating this book. I love you!

Violeta Meyners—You took the most perfect photo for this cover. Thank you for supporting me in bringing my vision to life.

Dawn—I am so blessed to have you in my life as a teacher. Your energy, wisdom, force, power, elegance, beauty and care have been such a soothing balm to my heart this past year. Thank you for loving me no matter what.

Mildred—I have felt your presence the past two years more than ever. Thank you for being my guardian angel when I've felt the most lonely, isolated and confused. Your transmission is undeniably powerful, and I'm proud to be of your blood.

Magdalene—You are a lighthouse for true embodied priesthood. What a blessing it is to share a name with you. Thank you for standing tall for us all as the "high tower" of devotional love.

ABOUT THE AUTHOR

Madelyn Moon is a leading voice in the world of feminine-masculine relationships, devoted to serving women in liberating their expressive, artistic hearts with themselves, with partners, and with the world. Her work and story has been featured in hundreds of podcasts as well as various publications such as BBC, The Huffington Post, Teen Vogue, Thought Catalog, Nylon Magazine, The Daily Mail, Vice, Greatist, Men's Health, PEOPLE and ABC News Nightline. Madelyn teaches live programs, workshops and courses both online and in person; you can find more of her work online at maddymoon.com and on Instagram @madelynmoon. She lives in Austin, Texas with her papillon, Ollie Gizmo Moon.

Printed in Great Britain
by Amazon

10464927R00181